CIVIL WAR ALMANAC

by Justin Segal

Illustrations by Ned Butterfield

LOWELL HOUSE JUVENILE

LOS ANGELES

CONTEMPORARY BOOKS

CHICAGO

For Raina, the best fighter I ever knew
—J.S.

PHOTO CREDITS

front cover: American Red Cross: Clara Barton; Library of Congress: Drummer Boys, Abraham Lincoln, Ruins at Richmond, Stars & Stripes; National Portrait Gallery, Smithsonian Institution: Frederick Douglass, General Robert E. Lee.

back cover: Library of Congress: Ulysses S. Grant.

insides: Library of Congress: pp. 24, 26, 27, 29, 30, 34, 35, 53, 54, 73, 76, 96, 99, 107, 108, 109; National Portrait Gallery, Smithsonian Institution: p. 32 (detail of Robert E. Lee), p. 33 (detail of William T. Sherman); Ohio Historical Society: p. 108 (Ulysses S. Grant).

President and Publisher: Jack Artenstein
Director of Publishing Services: Rena Copperman
Managing Editor, Juvenile Division: Lindsey Hay
Editor in Chief, Juvenile: Amy Downing
Editor: Jessica Oifer
Art Director: Lisa-Theresa Lenthall

Cover Design: Justin Segal
Text Design: Carolyn Wendt

Library of Congress Card Catalog Number: 97-3977

ISBN: 1-56565-586-9

Lowell House books can be purchased at special discounts when ordered in bulk for premiums and special sales. Contact Department TC at the following address:

Lowell House Juvenile
2020 Avenue of the Stars, Suite 300
Los Angeles, CA 90067

Manufactured in the United States of America

10 9 8 7 6 5 4 3 2

CONTENTS

INTRODUCTION
What Is a Civil War?..*4*

PRELUDE TO WAR
Life in the Civil War Era..*10*
North vs. South...*17*

THE WAR YEARS
The Leaders *24*
The Battles...*37*
The Soldiers...*47*
Spies & Secret Allies *63*
Women & the War *70*
Flags & Banners...*77*
Civil War Inventions *78*
The Home Front...*85*

AFTER THE WAR
Aftermath..*93*
A New America *103*
Civil War Legacies...*106*

THE CIVIL WAR & YOU
Books, Films & More..*116*
See the Civil War Yourself! *123*

CIVIL WAR CHRONOLOGY *124*

INDEX *128*

INTRODUCTION

On April 12, 1861, America went to war.

Like America's Revolutionary War, it was a struggle for freedom and independence.

But the American Revolution had been a war against Great Britain. This war was not a war against another country. For the first time in history, states in the North were battling states in the South. Americans were fighting against Americans. The country was torn apart by a struggle that would become known as the Civil War.

When the war was over, and America was put back together again, it was a very different place. It had been changed forever. America was stronger and freer than before the war, and it had been preserved as a single nation.

WHAT IS A CIVIL WAR?

America's Civil War was unlike any other war America has fought. It was a war in which soldiers on both sides belonged to the same nation, in which fathers fought against fathers and brothers battled against brothers. There are many reasons why America had a civil war. Though it was an unusual war for the United States, civil wars are quite common throughout the world.

THE BATTLE LINES ARE DRAWN

A civil war is a battle between a country's own citizens. Sometimes those citizens live in different states or territories, and other times they belong to different political groups.

In America's Civil War the battle line was drawn between the Northern and Southern states. The states in the North were called the Union (or the United States of America). States in the South were called the *Confederacy* (or the Confederate States of America). Union soldiers were called Yankees, and Confederate soldiers were called Rebels.

For four long years the Union and Confederacy fought. It was a battle between those who supported slavery and those who believed black people should be free. Rebels who wanted their states to leave the Union faced Yankees who believed the United States had to remain together.

CIVIL WAR WORDS

Confederacy: Any group of two or more states that work together for a common purpose can be called a confederacy. The Confederate States of America, generally known as the Confederacy, was organized in 1861. It consisted of 11 American states that wanted to leave the Union: Alabama, Arkansas, Florida, Georgia, Louisiana, Mississippi, North Carolina, South Carolina, Tennessee, Texas, and Virginia.

WHY AMERICA HAD A CIVIL WAR

There were many reasons why America had a civil war.

One reason was the Declaration of Independence, which was written in 1776. It proclaimed that "all men are created equal,"

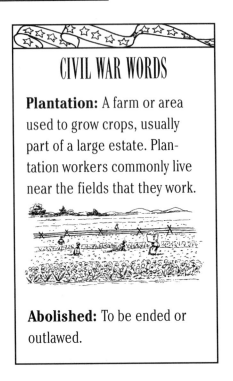

CIVIL WAR WORDS

Plantation: A farm or area used to grow crops, usually part of a large estate. Plantation workers commonly live near the fields that they work.

Abolished: To be ended or outlawed.

with a right to "life, liberty, and the pursuit of happiness." But America was a country with slaves, and people who were slaves were not free or equal at all. During the years leading up to the war, many Americans began to feel that the Declaration of Independence should also apply to slaves—namely, that slaves should be free, too.

America had existed with two kinds of states—slave states and free states—for many years. The states in the North were free states, and those in the South were slave states. The main reason for this was that Northern states had most of the nation's factories, while Southern states grew most of the country's

crops. These crops were grown on large *plantations* that used great numbers of slaves to tend to farm work.

Many people—especially those who lived in the North and didn't own any slaves—felt that this was wrong. These Northerners, who included some members of the United States government, believed that slave owners had no right to force black Americans to work on their farms. They believed all Americans should be able to live and work wherever they pleased.

The Southerners who owned slaves disliked the Northerners' desire to end slavery. They believed that if the government was going to end slavery, slave states should be able to leave the United States and form a new country for themselves. They thought the government had no right to decide what was right and wrong and wanted each state to govern itself. Other people thought that philosophy was wrong, and that no state should have the power to leave the Union.

While Americans in the North and South argued over slavery, the country continued to grow larger—adding territories that would one day become new states in the Union. Some people wanted these new states to be free states. Others wanted them to be slave states.

America had a civil war to decide these many issues. After it was over, slavery was *abolished,* all states became free states, and the United States was considered indivisible once and for all.

★ ★ ★ ★ ★ ★ ★ HOT WAR, COLD WAR ★ ★ ★ ★ ★ ★ ★

"The art of war is simple enough," Union general Ulysses S. Grant declared. "Find out where your enemy is. Get at him as soon as you can. Strike at him as hard as you can and as often as you can, and keep moving on." Warfare today, however, is not so simple. There are many different kinds of war:

HOT WAR: A hot war is any armed conflict between two or more nations. It usually causes the destruction of lives and territory.

COLD WAR: Sometimes called a "cold peace," a cold war describes two or more nations who are hostile toward each other without actually engaging in armed conflict.

PROXY WAR: A proxy war is an extension of a cold war. It is a battle between two or more combatants who are being supported with equipment from or training by other countries. This gives the outside countries an opportunity to test their weapons against each other without having to fight themselves.

CIVIL WAR: A war between two or more different groups or states within a single nation.

GUERRILLA WAR: A form of war usually carried on by a small group of rebels battling against an established foe, such as the government. The rebel soldiers, called guerrillas, often hide within mountains or jungles and attack the enemy with hit-and-run raids.

COVERT WAR: A type of war usually conducted by top-secret security or intelligence agencies (such as the CIA in the United States). A covert war often relies upon guerrilla fighters, and usually remains a secret from the public. Sometimes a government can conduct a covert war against its own people.

A WAR OF ATTRITION: A war designed to slowly force an enemy into submission, rather than engaging in direct combat. Tactics include use of blockades and other ways to cut off an enemy's communications or food supply. Many types of war can become a war of attrition, as attrition becomes a strategy used in addition to regular combat.

NUCLEAR WAR: A war in which two or more combatants use nuclear weapons to destroy the enemy. It is believed this type of war could destroy all human civilization.

HOW COMMON IS CIVIL WAR?

America is not the only country to have fought a civil war. There have been many civil wars in our world, each fought for different reasons and in different ways. Some countries, like North and South Korea—who fought a full-scale civil war against each other from 1950–1953—have been fighting a kind of cold civil war ever since. In other countries, such as China, outbreaks of civil protest are so quickly defeated by the government that a rebellion doesn't have a chance to become a full-scale war.

Other civil wars in the twentieth century include:

- Russian-Chechnyan Civil War (1995–1996)
- Bosnian-Herzegovinian Civil War (1992–1995)
- Lebanese Civil War (1975–1990)

- Spanish Civil War (1936–1939)
- Russian Civil War (1918–1920)

★ ★ ★ ★ ★ DON'T CALL IT THE CIVIL WAR ★ ★ ★ ★ ★

While it was being fought, the Civil War wasn't actually called by that name. Americans had many different reasons for going to war, so different people used different names to describe the conflict, depending upon what they were fighting for:

★ The War Between the States
★ The Second American Revolution
★ The Confederate War
★ The Southern Rebellion
★ The War for Southern Independence
★ The Second War for Independence
★ The War for Constitutional Liberty
★ The War for State's Rights
★ The War for Separation
★ The War Against Slavery
★ The Brothers' War
★ Mr. Lincoln's War
★ The War of the North and South
★ The War of the Southern Planters

It wasn't until the 1870s, years after the war was over, that people first began using the term the Civil War. This is because the North won the war. From the Northern perspective, Southern states had no right to leave the Union, so the war had been between states that were all in the same country. The battle had been a civil war.

But the Confederate states believed they had already left the Union before the war began, and were a separate country fighting against the United States. If the Confederacy had won the war, it probably would not be called the Civil War today. Instead, it might be known as The War Between the States or The Second American Revolution.

★ ★

9

PRELUDE TO WAR

America's Civil War began on April 12, 1861, but the events that caused the war started much earlier in the nation's history. Americans had been arguing about whether slavery was right or wrong for hundreds of years. When no compromise could be found, people began to talk of war.

LIFE IN THE CIVIL WAR ERA

Everyday life in the mid-1800s was very different from life today. It took a long time to travel from one place to another. Mail was delivered on horseback, and the fastest it could be sent across the country was almost two weeks. Children worked from a young age, and they were lucky if they could go to school at all.

SCHOOL DAYS

During this time period, schooling was unlike education today. Many children lived and worked at home during the day, helping their families. They were taught by their parents or other relatives in the evening. Sometimes they even had to teach themselves to read or write.

Other children were able to go to school, but learning in the classroom was sometimes much harder than studying at home. There was usually just one teacher for a whole region, so classes had students of many different ages all together in a single room. Different students studied different lessons. Some knew how to read and write, and some did not. Everybody recited his or her own lessons aloud at the same time, which made the schoolrooms very noisy.

If things got too noisy, or a pupil lagged behind in his or her learning, teachers were allowed to hit the students with a stick or a ruler. Some teachers called these sticks their "board of education."

Most children learned to read from the same book, *McGuffey's* Eclectic *Reader,* which was first published in 1836. It was a book that told a number of stories, and then listed all the new and important words the children should learn in each story.

CIVIL WAR WORDS

Eclectic: Something made of material, words, or ideas from many different sources.

TRAVEL BY HORSE AND BUGGY

It was difficult for citizens to travel very far during the Civil War era. Ordinary people traveled only when necessary, and more often than not they spent most of their time at home.

Traveling by road was a bumpy, tiring, and sometimes dangerous experience. Roads were made from dirt or mud, and horse-drawn carriages could sometimes get stuck or be overturned on the uneven surfaces.

When people did travel, they often went by waterway. Steamboats carried passengers along the Mississippi, Ohio, and Missouri rivers, as well as through the *canals* connecting the Great Lakes to the Atlantic Ocean. Sometimes people traveled on wide wooden rafts called flatboats, which were propelled forward with a long pole pushed against the river bottom.

CIVIL WAR WORDS

Canal: A man-made waterway built to transport people and supplies where no natural river exists.

In the decade just before the Civil War, however, travel conditions did begin to improve. Private companies leased many of the roads and they made them smoother and safer, charging travelers a fee to use them. The biggest improvement came with the spread of railroads. Tracks were laid along the entire east coast of the United States and quickly spread further inland, connecting roads and waterways—and people—everywhere.

VISITING THE PRESIDENT'S HOUSE

Before the Civil War began, any American citizen could visit the White House and ask to meet or speak with the president.

Three poor young girls who lived nearby once wandered into the White House during a fancy presidential gathering. Their dresses were old, dirty, and torn, and the girls were amazed by the elegant decorations they saw. Suddenly they bumped into President Lincoln himself—a tall fatherly figure dressed in black.

The girls turned to run away, but President Lincoln said, "Little girls! Are you going to pass me without shaking hands?"

They stopped and looked at their president in amazement. He bent down and politely shook each one of their hands. They may have been poor, but they were welcome in the president's house.

Today, people can visit the White House and tour several rooms on display, but only special invited guests are allowed to meet with the president himself.

THE SLAVE OWNER WHO WAS BLACK

Believe it or not, not all slave owners were white. A Louisiana farmer named Andrew Durnford once owned 77 slaves . . . even though he was black!

Unlike most black Americans in the early 1800s, Andrew Durnford was born free. His father had been an English aristocrat before moving to the United States, and Andrew was wealthy enough to buy his own sugar plantation. At age 28 he bought his first slave, Noel. Then, within a year, he purchased 18 more.

Durnford spent as little money as possible, so he fed his slaves only as much as they needed to have the strength to work his plantation. Even though he said freed slaves should have the opportunity to move back to Africa, he freed only four of his own slaves in his lifetime and purchased many more.

But Durnford did care about the slaves he owned, and he thought about their futures. After he died, his slaves were freed, and they inherited some of his money to use for a proper education.

THE DAY THE POST OFFICE FREED A SLAVE

Southern slaves yearning for freedom sometimes tried daring and dangerous escapes.

One escaped slave from Richmond, Virginia, was nicknamed Henry "Box" Brown, because he said God had told him to escape to freedom in a box. Henry built a large box similar to those used for shipping plantation crops and drilled some small air holes in it. He marked "this side up with care" on the outside and crawled inside the box with some water to drink. The box

★ ★ ★ ★ ★ ★ ★ ★ ★ ★ ★

LOST: SLAVE— REWARD!

In the century leading up to the Civil War, the institution of slavery had become so commonplace that many traders placed ads in newspapers to buy and sell their slaves. "Lost and Found" sections listed runaway slaves and offered rewards for their return.

★ ★ ★ ★ ★ ★ ★ ★ ★ ★ ★

was addressed to a post office in Philadelphia, Pennsylvania— free territory for a black person. Soon enough the plantation owner shipped the parcel off, unaware that his slave Henry— instead of crops—was inside.

At the postal depot near his plantation, Henry's box was dropped to the ground, upside down. As blood rushed to his head, Henry's eyes felt as if they would explode. He considered calling for help but didn't. More than anything else, Henry Brown wanted to be a free man, even if he died trying.

Finally, after days of travel, the box reached its Philadelphia destination. When it was opened, Henry stood up. With the blood pumping inside his head, he fainted before he could get a glimpse of his new home. Fortunately, his condition was not serious, and he awoke a short while later, a Pennsylvania citizen and a free man at last!

THE PONY EXPRESS

America's mail carriers have always prided themselves on delivering the mail under any condition, but never was their job as difficult—and dangerous—as during the era of the Pony Express.

In the pre-Civil War years, the vast territory stretching to the Pacific Coast was being settled by new pioneers, but there was no reliable way to send information coast-to-coast. The *Transcontinental Railroad,* the first railroad to link the entire country, would not be completed until several years after the war, in 1869.

Thus, in 1860, the Pony Express was created. It was America's first high-speed communications service. Messengers had to ride through miles of rugged terrain and hostile Indian territory to deliver the mail. Advertisements for horsemen asked for "young, expert riders, willing to face death daily. Orphans preferred."

Pony Express riders lived lives of daring adventure. "Buffalo Bill" Cody once rode for 322 miles without stopping after discovering his relief rider had been killed by Indians. "Pony Bob" Haslam made the trip with rags in his mouth to stop the bleeding from an Indian attack. One Pony Express horse even delivered the mail by itself after its rider had been killed along the way!

In 1861, however, only a year and a half after it began, the Pony Express era was over. A cheaper, faster, safer way to deliver news coast-to-coast had been devised: the transcontinental telegraph, which used electrical wires to send messages across the wide American continent.

CIVIL WAR WORDS

Transcontinental Railroad: The first railway to travel the entire length of the United States, from the Atlantic Ocean to the Pacific Ocean. Construction on the Transcontinental Railroad began in 1865 and was completed on May 10, 1869. The thousands of miles of tunnels and tracks needed to build the railroad were laid by Chinese and Irish immigrants working for $1 a day.

THE BIRTH OF BLOOMERS

Life in the Civil War era was bound by strict rules of etiquette. All ladies were expected to wear hoopskirts, which were large, billowing dresses. But hoopskirts were difficult to walk in and even more difficult to maneuver through doorways. One woman decided to protest having to wear the uncomfortable skirts—and accidentally created a new fashion craze in the process!

Amelia Bloomer liked to protest many things. She regularly wrote articles for her hometown newspaper about the dangers of alcohol and other vices. In particular, she disliked the extremes of modern fashion. To protest the ridiculousness of the hoopskirt, Amelia decided to parade through town in a garment she thought equally preposterous: a billowing sort of trouser cut short at the knees.

The outfit caused an immediate scandal. Most people were horrified by the unladylike garments, but feminists hailed them as clothes that could free women from wearing large, billowing dresses. The newspapers dubbed the fashion bloomers, and women have worn them to this very day.

DID YOU KNOW...

There's No Indian on an Indian-Head Penny?

Everybody knows that Abraham Lincoln is pictured on America's one-cent coin, and some may know that before the Lincoln penny was issued, the Indian-head penny was the common currency . . . but did you know that there is no Indian on the Indian-head penny?

When the United States Treasury decided to issue the first penny—in 1859—the U.S. Mint's engraver, James B. Longacre, needed an appropriate image for the front of the coin. He settled on a profile of Liberty, a fictional woman who symbolized America's peace and freedom. Because feather bonnets were popular at the time, Longacre decided to put one atop Liberty's head.

But when people saw the new coin, they thought the bonnet was a feather headdress. The only people who wore feather headdresses were Indians. The Liberty cent became known as the Indian-head penny from that point on.

THINGS THAT HAVE STAYED THE SAME

Not everything during the time of the Civil War was different from life today. Blue jeans were a popular fashion even then, families watched baseball games together, and children chomped on chewing gum. Roller skating, chess, and billiards were invented. The first department store chains were built in the cities, and theaters introduced modern conveniences like air-conditioning for the first time.

NORTH VS. SOUTH

The tensions between Northerners and Southerners grew rapidly in the years preceding the Civil War. Arguments over slavery arose each time a new state or territory was added to the Union. The nation was not yet at war, but the battle of words was growing worse. It was getting harder and harder to work out a compromise and keep the nation at peace.

AMERICA'S GROWING PROBLEM

In the 1850s Americans enjoyed a time of rapid growth and opportunity. Southern plantations provided fuel used by Northern factories. Northern industry produced goods such as paper and bars of soap that supplied the South. "The two halves of this Union," said Missouri senator Thomas Hart Benton, "were made for each other as much as Adam and Eve."

During his administration President James Polk spoke about creating an "empire for liberty." His vision was called Manifest Destiny. It meant that Americans were destined to settle land all the way from the Atlantic to the Pacific Ocean. In just a few years Florida, Texas, Iowa, Wisconsin, and California joined the Union, and Polk's vision became a reality.

Americans were eager to move into the new territories, but with the admission of each new state, the question of slavery reignited. Southerners wanted new territories to be slave states, and Northerners wanted them to be free. The faster America spread westward, the more Northerners and Southerners felt they were parts of two very different Americas. They stopped working together and began to talk of war instead.

THE SOUTHERN WAY OF LIFE

In spite of the cruel ownership of slaves, the traditional image of the South was one of grace and civility.

Southern plantation owners liked to see themselves as courtly gentlemen, tending to their kingdoms. Wealthy Southern women dressed elegantly and hosted elaborate parties in their mansions. They had black servants attending to their every need.

Southern gentlemen treated each other with respect. They believed in studying the art of war and hunting on horseback. They considered themselves a peaceful people. Only Southern gentlemen, said Mississippi plantation owner Jefferson Davis, "go to a military academy [without intending] to follow the profession of arms."

Few Southerners wanted their way of life to change. One Southerner explained, "We want no manufactures; we desire no trading, no mechanical or manufacturing classes. As long as we have our rice, our sugar, our tobacco, and our cotton, we can command wealth to purchase all we want."

Without slaves to produce their crops, however, the Southern way of life would vanish forever. Protecting the Southern way of life—by preserving slavery and maintaining courtly traditions—soon became known as the Southern cause.

THE NORTHERN WAY OF LIFE

Life in the North was very different from that in the South. Instead of farms and plantations, most Northern states had factories. In fact, Northern industries were responsible for manufacturing nearly *all* the goods—from sugar to household tools to shoes—for the nation. The North also built the country's ships and railroads, which transported these goods to the rest of the country and overseas.

Northern cities were noisy, busy places. Nearly 3 million new people came to America in the decade before the war. Most of these immigrants lived in the North because the Northern cities were growing rapidly and there were many jobs available there. Unlike people in the South, these immigrants were not interested in preserving an established way of life. They were devoted to building a new America, where everybody had an opportunity to work and prosper. They learned to live and work together, accepting each other's various nationalities as a diversity that made America strong.

Promoting this sense of prosperity, fighting to bring equal opportunities to *all* Americans, and keeping the Union together came to be known as the Northern cause.

THE MISSOURI COMPROMISE

In March 1820, when the citizens of Missouri applied for admission to the Union as a slave state, there were 11 slave states and 11 free states already in the Union. Most congress-men did not want to upset the balance of power by allowing there to be more states of one kind than another.

When Maine requested admission to the Union as a free state, shortly thereafter, a compromise was made: Both states were allowed to join the Union at the same time. This agreement became known as the Missouri Compromise.

★ ★ ★ ★ **SLAVERY ABOLISHED ... IN 1652!** ★ ★ ★ ★

Even though slavery wasn't abolished in America until the Civil War ended in 1865, the slave trade—bringing new slaves to the country from overseas—was outlawed by Congress in 1808. What's more, the colony of Rhode Island outlawed the institution of slavery in 1652 . . . 124 years before the United States signed the Declaration of Independence!

★ ★

THE COMPROMISE OF 1850

As the debate over slavery grew, congressmen tried to pass new laws that would satisfy people in the North and the South. Together, these laws became known as the Compromise of 1850.

To show support for people who opposed slavery, the Compromise of 1850 allowed California into the Union as a free state and declared slavery illegal in the District of Columbia, home of the nation's capital. To satisfy those who believed in slavery, the new laws increased penalties on people who helped runaway slaves. It also allowed citizens in the Utah and New Mexico territories to vote on whether they would be free or slave states when they joined the Union.

The Compromise of 1850 did little to solve the growing crisis over slavery, but many historians believe that if it had not been passed, the Civil War may have begun years sooner.

THE DRED SCOTT DECISION

In 1857 the U.S. Supreme Court issued a ruling that the justices believed would resolve the issue of slavery at last.

In 1834 an Army surgeon and Missouri slave owner named John Emerson took his slave Dred Scott with him on assignment to military outposts in Illinois and the Wisconsin Territory— two places where slavery was illegal. Emerson and Scott returned to Missouri four years later.

When John Emerson died in 1843, antislavery lawyers offered to help Dred Scott sue the surviving Emerson family for his freedom. They argued that his years spent living in free-state territory had already made him a free man.

The Supreme Court agreed to hear the case in 1856 and announced its verdict the following year. In the decision it was ruled that slaves were to be considered property, and every slaveholder had the right to transport personal property with him as he traveled between states, even between free states. A black man had "no rights which any white man was bound to respect."

If the justices had set out to end the slave crisis with their ruling, they succeeded only in making things worse. Southern slaveholders claimed victory in the struggle, and Northerners grew more determined to abolish slavery than ever before. Meanwhile, the Emerson family decided to free Dred Scott, who found paying work as a luggage porter at a St. Louis, Missouri, hotel. He died in 1858.

BLEEDING KANSAS

The first *real* battle over the issues that sparked the Civil War began in 1854 and raged for seven years in the territory that came to be known as Bleeding Kansas.

When proslavery senator Stephen A. Douglas introduced the Kansas-Nebraska Act of 1854 in Congress, he proposed dividing the large Nebraska Territory into two separate states, Kansas and Nebraska. Each would be allowed to join the United States as a free or a slave state by popular vote of each state's citizens.

Soon after the Act was proposed, residents of other Southern states moved to the Kansas Territory, hoping to gather enough support to bring Kansas into the Union as a slave state. To counter them, other people moved in from the North, urging citizens to make Kansas a free state.

In 1855, when an election was called, hundreds of pro-slavery citizens from Missouri rushed to Kansas to prevent Free Staters from voting by threatening them. After the election, the proslavery forces declared victory and drafted a constitution making Kansas a slave state. But the Free Staters declared the election a fraud and elected a legislature of their own.

Almost immediately, the two groups began to fight, burning each other's homes and destroying each other's crops.

Each side wanted to force the other to leave the territory. Within a year over 200 people had been killed.

Finally, after seven years of fighting, the battle of Bleeding Kansas ended. In 1861, after the Civil War had begun, the Union needed all the help it could muster, so President Lincoln admitted Kansas to the United States—a free state at last.

"THE LITTLE WOMAN WHO MADE THIS BIG WAR"

Few people had as big an impact on the growing debate over slavery than Harriet Beecher Stowe, who wrote an antislavery book called *Uncle Tom's Cabin* in 1852.

Stowe, a minister's daughter, taught black students at a Cincinnati, Ohio, school (most black Americans who lived in the North were free citizens). But she wanted to do something to end the cruelty and mistreatment of all black Americans. Her sister-in-law wrote to her: "If I could use the pen as you can, I would write something which would make this whole nation feel what an accursed thing slavery is." Stowe set out to do just that.

Based on a short story she had written for the abolitionist newspaper *National Era, Uncle Tom's Cabin* shows what life was like for slaves living on a plantation. It is the first American novel to have a black hero, a slave named Uncle Tom who is cruelly mistreated by his white owner, Simon Legree. The book changed the way many Americans felt about slavery. People in the North began to say that it was worth going to war to free the slaves in the South.

Harriet Beecher Stowe was introduced to President Lincoln in 1862, two years after the war began. "So," the President said as he shook the schoolteacher's hand, "this is the little woman who made this big war."

In all, *Uncle Tom's Cabin* sold 300,000 copies in its first year. As of today it has been translated into 37 languages worldwide.

23

THE WAR YEARS

When the fighting erupted at Fort Sumter, South Carolina, the Civil War had begun at last. With it came a new era in America's history, introducing new leaders, innovative weapons, and improved fighting techniques. Women and blacks became involved in the struggle as they had in no previous war.

THE LEADERS

The declaration of war did more than divide the nation between North and South. It divided the people themselves. As they chose sides, men who had been friends became bitter fighting enemies. Generals who trained together at West Point Military Academy suddenly found themselves leading opposing armies. Both the Union and the Confederacy found leaders to champion their cause.

ABRAHAM LINCOLN
PRESIDENT OF THE UNITED STATES

More than any other person from the Civil War, Abraham Lincoln spoke the words that most Americans remember today. "A house divided against itself cannot stand," he said. "I believe this government cannot endure permanently half slave and half free." Lincoln was a self-educated country boy born in a log cabin in Kentucky, but he was known for speaking in a simple way that people could understand, whether or not they agreed with his views.

In 1858 Lincoln ran for Congress against proslavery candidate Stephen A. Douglas. The two men debated the issue of slavery. "As I would not be a *slave*," said Lincoln, "so I would not be a *master*. This expresses my idea of democracy." Lincoln lost the election, but he gained fame for his ability to defend the Union cause. Two years later the two men competed for the presidency. This time Lincoln won the election, becoming America's 16th leader.

Because of his numerous speeches against slavery, most Southerners expected President Lincoln to free the slaves when he became president. Rather than let their slaves go free, South Carolina and 10 other Southern states decided to *secede* from the nation. They called themselves the Con-federate States of America.

CIVIL WAR WORDS

Secede: To formally withdraw membership in an organization or political group.

But President Lincoln had no plans to outlaw slavery overnight. While he didn't approve of slavery, he felt it was part of the Southern life and hoped it would be erased gradually over a number of years. In fact, when the South seceded from the Union, Lincoln felt his chief duty was not to abolish slavery but to hold the Union together.

Lincoln knew there were Federal troops in various forts along the southern coastline, including Fort Sumter in Charleston Harbor, South Carolina. When South Carolina declared itself a separate country, these troops were suddenly in enemy territory, cut off from the rest of the Union. Lincoln proclaimed a peaceful mission to bring food to the trapped Union soldiers. "No bloodshed," he promised, "unless it is forced upon the government." But then, on April 12, 1861, the Confederate Army fired upon Fort Sumter. The Civil War had begun.

DID YOU KNOW...

Lincoln's Hair Stylist Was an 11-Year-Old Girl?

Abraham Lincoln has one of the best-known faces in America's history, but did you know he didn't grow his famous beard until just before the Civil War? On October 18, 1860, while running for president, he received a letter from an 11-year-old girl named Grace Bedell, which said, "I have got four brothers and part of them will vote for you any way and if you let your whiskers grow I will try and get the rest of them to vote for you; you would look a great deal better for your face is so thin . . . All the ladies like whiskers and they would tease their husbands to vote for you and then you would be President."

Although he wasn't sure it was a good idea to change his appearance while running for president, Lincoln took Grace's advice and began growing the short black beard for which he soon became famous. When he traveled to her hometown, Lincoln thanked Grace Bedell for her suggestion.

At the outset, Lincoln had difficulty finding a general who could win the war for him. He tried many different generals—Winfield Scott, George B. McClellan, Ambrose Burnside, Joseph Hooker, George G. Meade. He even served as his own battle commander at times. Finally, he appointed General Ulysses S. Grant and General William Tecumseh Sherman. They were men who could fight aggressively, the way Lincoln wanted. The tide of war began to turn for the Union.

As victory became more certain, Lincoln realized the war gave him the power to outlaw slavery after all. In 1863 he issued the Emancipation Proclamation, which declared all Southern slaves free and allowed blacks in the North—who were already free—to join the Union Army. "This nation, under God," Lincoln declared, "shall have a new birth of freedom."

In 1864 Lincoln was reelected, and he began to look ahead to how he might reunite the nation after the war. He was sensitive to Southern feelings and wanted the war wounds to heal quickly. Some Southerners, however, did not want peace. Six days after the war ended, a Southerner named John Wilkes Booth assassinated the president in the name of the Confederate cause.

America had lost one of its greatest visionary leaders. Lincoln, himself, foresaw his fate. "When the hour comes for dealing with slavery," he said, "I trust I will be willing to do my duty though it cost my life."

JEFFERSON DAVIS
CONFEDERATE PRESIDENT

In many ways Jefferson Davis, president of the Confederacy, was similar to U.S. president Abraham Lincoln. Like Lincoln, he was born in a small log cabin in Kentucky. During the Black Hawk War of 1832, he volunteered for a regiment of untrained recruits, which was led by Lincoln for a brief time. And as he grew into adulthood Davis became a tall, dramatic-looking figure known for his honesty, his honor, and his determination to follow through on his promises, very much like Lincoln.

Of course, Jefferson Davis was also very different from Lincoln. Lincoln had almost no experience with slavery before the presidency, whereas Jefferson Davis owned slaves on his plantation in Mississippi. Unlike Lincoln, Davis had been professionally trained as a soldier at West Point Military Academy. During the Mexican War (1846–1848), while Lincoln worked as a lawyer in Springfield, Illinois, Davis became a military hero. After the war, Davis's fame helped him win a seat in the U.S. Congress, whereas Lincoln lost his own race for Congress to Illinois senator Stephen Douglas in 1858.

In the Senate, Davis argued for laws to preserve slavery and the Southern way of life. He also championed the spread of slavery into new states that might join America in the future. Most of all, Davis believed in each state's right to secede from the Union. When Lincoln's election to the presidency made it clear that slavery would one day be abolished, Jefferson Davis decided he was the best man to lead the Confederate cause. "All we ask," he declared in the name of the Rebels, "is to be left alone."

Almost immediately, Davis was faced with the difficult task of not just winning a war but founding a new nation—the Confederate States of America. He soon realized that he understood military strategy better than governing and economics. From the start of the war, his soldiers lacked proper food and supplies. Each of the Southern states felt they could do what seemed best for their own soldiers, instead of what President Davis wanted. After years of struggle, the problems became unbeatable and the Rebel government collapsed in defeat.

Davis lived in *exile,* in Canada, working for an insurance company after the war. When President Andrew Johnson issued a full *pardon* to the Confederate leadership, on Christmas Day in 1868, Davis returned to America, living out the final years of his life in Mississippi. In 1881 he published a book called *The Rise and Fall of the Confederate Government,* in which he blamed his army generals for the failure of the Southern cause.

Jefferson Davis did not regret his role in America's Civil War. "Tell the world," he said to a reporter, "that I only loved America."

CIVIL WAR WORDS

Exile: Being banished, usually by the government, from one's native country or home and forbidden to return. Sometimes people exile themselves, abandoning their countries by their own choice.

Pardon: To forgive or excuse a person from punishment for crimes they have committed.

WINFIELD SCOTT
UNION GENERAL

At the outbreak of the Civil War, General Winfield Scott had served in the U.S. Army for over 50 years, and was the commanding officer of the Union Army. He was 75 years old, however, and suffered from a disease called *gout,* which forced him to spend much of his time in bed. Even when he could get out of bed, Scott was so overweight that he could no longer ride a horse. But his mind and military skills remained as strong as ever.

Scott devised a plan to win the war by cutting off the Southern states' trade with Europe, where they could get vital military supplies. He proposed sending Union troops into the South from areas to the north and the west, and squeeze the Confederacy into submission. General Scott thought his plan would take two or three years to succeed.

CIVIL WAR WORDS

Gout: A disease of the blood that causes severe pain in the hands and feet, and swelling in the big toe and joints.

Most Northerners laughed when they heard the old general's plan, instead expecting victory in a matter of months. They called Scott's strategy the Anaconda Plan, after the large snake that slowly squeezes its victims to death. But President Lincoln knew General Scott was a wise military strategist. In 1835 Scott had written *Infantry Tactics,* the first complete manual of military strategy for the U.S. Army. Even so, Lincoln needed to rally more Northern support for his war effort and decided to appoint a new general to lead the Union army, the younger and more popular General George B. McClellan.

As it turned out, the Union Army followed Winfield Scott's plan exactly, and it did lead to victory—though the war lasted four years instead of the three he had predicted. Perhaps if the wise old general had remained in charge, things might have ended more quickly.

ULYSSES S. GRANT
UNION GENERAL

Ulysses S. Grant was born in an Ohio town called Point Pleasant—a fitting home for a shy, quiet boy with a gentle nature.

His original name was Hiram Ulysses Grant, but Grant hated the initials H.U.G. and called himself Ulysses Hiram Grant instead. When he was 17, he entered West Point Military Academy. There his name was accidentally listed as Ulysses Simpson Grant. Grant decided to keep the new name and became Ulysses S. Grant from that point on.

In 1846 Grant served in the Mexican War (1846–1848). An excellent soldier, he understood battle strategy and was eager to fight. After the war, he was assigned to a small *outpost* in California. It was lonely duty, and he was unhappy. In 1854 he decided to resign from the military and start his own business. Grant tried farming and selling real estate, but neither business succeeded. With no other choice, he went back home to Ohio and worked in his father's leather store. At age 38 Grant felt his life had been a failure.

CIVIL WAR WORDS

Outpost: A small station away from the headquarters or main part of an army, usually on the frontier.

Then the Civil War started. The Union needed every experienced soldier it had, and Grant was recommissioned as a colonel. His fighting spirit revived. People took notice of his success on the battlefield, and within two months he was promoted to general. Grant was "the quietest little fellow you ever saw," said President Lincoln. "But he fights."

When word spread that General Grant refused to negotiate a truce before a battle was won, he earned the nickname Unconditional Surrender. The shy boy from Ohio had become a symbol of the Union's determination to win the war at any cost. In 1866, after he led the Union Army to victory, Grant was promoted to general of the entire army—the first active commander to hold that rank since George Washington.

★ ★ ★ ★ ★ ★ ★ **WHAT'S YOUR RANK?** ★ ★ ★ ★ ★ ★ ★

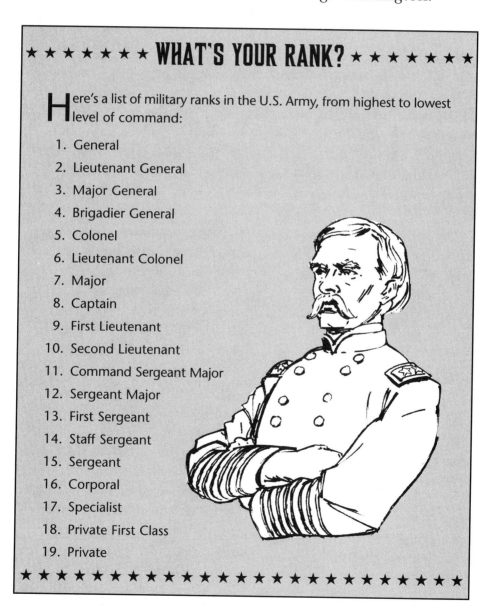

Here's a list of military ranks in the U.S. Army, from highest to lowest level of command:

1. General
2. Lieutenant General
3. Major General
4. Brigadier General
5. Colonel
6. Lieutenant Colonel
7. Major
8. Captain
9. First Lieutenant
10. Second Lieutenant
11. Command Sergeant Major
12. Sergeant Major
13. First Sergeant
14. Staff Sergeant
15. Sergeant
16. Corporal
17. Specialist
18. Private First Class
19. Private

★ ★

ROBERT E. LEE
CONFEDERATE GENERAL

Robert E. Lee was born into a Virginia family with a proud military history. His father, Henry Lee, commonly known as "Light-Horse Harry," had fought in the American Revolution and been a close friend of George Washington. But Lee's father died when he was a boy, and his family struggled for many years to make ends meet.

Because he had no money to pay for college, Lee decided to enroll in West Point Military Academy. He was a natural soldier, well liked and respected by his fellow cadets. During the Mexican War (1846–1848) General Winfield Scott, the commanding general, called Lee "the very best soldier I ever saw."

In February 1861, when seven Southern states—South Carolina, Georgia, Florida, Alabama, Mississippi, Louisiana, and Texas—declared themselves the Confederate States of America, Lee was summoned to military headquarters in Washington, D.C. He was asked to lead the Northern army and force the Rebel states to return to the Union. But Lee was from Virginia, a Southern slave state, and felt he could not attack his friends in the South. Then, in April 1861, Virginia, North Carolina, Tennessee, and Arkansas also declared their secession. Lee decided to return to Virginia and fight for the Southern cause.

CIVIL WAR WORDS

Provisions: Stocks of food and other supplies stored for future use.

From the outset of the war, it was clear that the South was vastly outnumbered. The Union Army had more troops, more ammunition, more weapons, and more *provisions* for their soldiers than the South, and a Northern blockade of Southern ports made their situation worse. Lee soldiered well and did everything he could to keep the Union Army from invading the Confederate capital in Richmond, Virginia. But as the years of battle took their toll, he lost too many soldiers and realized that Southern defeat was inevitable. Lee surrendered the Confederate Army to Union general Ulysses S. Grant at Appomattox Court House, Virginia, on April 9, 1865.

WILLIAM TECUMSEH SHERMAN
UNION MAJOR GENERAL

William Tecumseh Sherman was a fighting man. He was tall, with rough features and messy hair, and he looked like a gunfighter from the Wild West. But Sherman came from a family of lawyers and politicians, not outdoorsmen. His father was an Ohio Supreme Court justice, and his brother was a U.S. senator. He was orphaned at nine years old, and his foster father, Thomas Ewing, was also a U.S. senator. Still, Sherman didn't want to be a politician. He enrolled in West Point Military Academy instead.

Sherman served in the Mexican War (1846–1848), and later ran a military academy in Alexandria, Louisiana. When Louisiana seceded from the Union in 1861, Sherman was asked to join the Confederacy as a Rebel Army officer. He refused.

At first, he wanted to avoid helping either side in the conflict. Even though he didn't believe in slavery, Sherman felt it was firmly established in the Southern way of life and couldn't be outlawed without destroying the nation. But he also believed that no state had the right to leave the Union. Sherman eventually joined the Union Army as a colonel and was quickly promoted to brigadier general. He was a popular commander, talking nonstop, giving rapid-fire orders, and sending an endless stream of messages back to headquarters as he moved his troops forward into battle. To his men, General

Sherman was just Uncle Billy, but to General Grant he was a trusted ally, the second most important person in the Union war campaign.

Sherman led his army on a historic march through Georgia and the Carolinas, capturing and destroying weapons, farms, railways, and anything else that might be of use to the enemy. He even set the city of Atlanta, Georgia, on fire. Most Northerners considered him an avenging angel. In the South, though, Sherman was called the devil himself.

After the war, when Ulysses S. Grant was elected President of the United States, Sherman assumed command of the entire army. People began to talk of electing Sherman president himself one day. But during the war, Sherman's favorite son, William Tecumseh, Jr., had died from typhoid fever. "With Willy," the general explained, "dies in me all real ambition." He refused to accept the nomination.

THOMAS J. "STONEWALL" JACKSON
CONFEDERATE GENERAL

Throughout his life Thomas J. Jackson never felt comfortable around other people. He was serious, silent, and kept mostly to himself. He believed in discipline in all things. In fact, while a teacher at the Virginia Military Institute, Jackson was so strict about maintaining school rules that his students, who hated discipline, called him Tom Fool. Yet it was these qualities that made Jackson a legend as a military leader, and one of the best-known and most-feared generals in the Civil War.

From his first Civil War battle at Falling Waters, Virginia, where Jackson was unfazed by a large cannonball that smashed into a tree near his head, the general earned a reputation for fearlessness in battle. In fact, at the Battle of

Manassas—called Bull Run in the North—Confederate general Barnard Bee tried to reassure his frightened troops by saying, "There is Jackson, standing like a stone wall!" This nickname stuck, and Jackson became known as Stonewall Jackson. His reputation soon grew so big that Northern children who misbehaved were told by their mothers, "Be good or Stonewall will get you!"

Throughout the early war years Jackson seemed unbeatable, winning many battles against armies larger than his own, and marching his troops further and faster than any general had ever done before.

★ ★ ★ ★ ★ ★ ★ ★ ★ ★ ★ ★

A JACKSON FOR THE NORTH

Thomas "Stonewall" Jackson may have been one of the Confederacy's most famous leaders, but his sister Laura remained loyal to the Union throughout the war. She even sent a message to a Union soldier offering to become a nurse, promising to "take care of Federals as fast as brother Thomas would wound them."

★ ★ ★ ★ ★ ★ ★ ★ ★ ★ ★ ★

In 1863, however, while in the thick of battle at Chancellorsville, Virginia, Jackson was accidentally shot and wounded by one of his own men. He tried to fight on and rallied his troops as he had done a thousand times before, shouting, "Prepare for action." But his wounds were too great, and Jackson died on the battlefield.

GEORGE ARMSTRONG CUSTER
UNION GENERAL

Many people today know the name of General George Armstrong Custer from his defeat by the Sioux

Indians at Little Big Horn in 1876, often called Custer's Last Stand. Custer's military career began much earlier, however, when, in 1861, at age 22, he graduated last (with the worst grades) in his class from West Point Military Academy.

Custer may have done poorly in academic studies, but he proved to be ready for real-life battle. Throughout the Civil War he served with a wild fighting spirit for which he became famous. He lead the 3rd Cavalry Division wearing a trademark Wild West uniform of his own design. After helping to defeat Confederate general Jeb Stuart at the Battle of Gettysburg (July 1–3, 1863), his reputation grew as a daring and unpredictable opponent—one who sometimes ignored his own commanding officers in order to achieve victory on the battlefield.

After the Civil War, Custer remained in the military, successfully leading the 7th Cavalry during the Indian Wars (which were fought as the United States expanded westward, forcing Native Americans from their own land onto designated *Indian reservations*). But his lasting fame was to come from his defeat by Chiefs Sitting Bull and Crazy Horse at the Battle of Little Big Horn in Montana.

Oddly, Custer, who the Sioux called Long Hair because of his wild flowing locks, had cut off his hair just before riding into his last battle. None of his cavalry survived to explain why he had changed his trademark hairstyle.

CIVIL WAR WORDS

Indian reservation:
Government-owned land set aside for a tribe, or several tribes, of Indians to live on. The first reservation was created in 1646, when European immigrants in Massachusetts designated 6,000 acres of land exclusively for Indians who were willing to live peacefully with white settlers. Today there are more than 300 official Indian reservations spread across the continental United States.

THE BATTLES

The outcome of the Civil War was not decided by a single battle, but by scores of battles, large and small. Some battles involved hundreds of thousands of soldiers, fighting for days at a time. Other battles were small hit-and-run raids made by just a few men. For four long years, the war was fought on the ocean and the nation's rivers, and spread to the railways and the vast, scarcely populated west.

EDMUND RUFFIN, THE MAN WHO STARTED THE CIVIL WAR

Edmund Ruffin believed in the Southern way of life. He was a Virginia native and a wealthy plantation owner. He had worked hard to improve Southern agriculture, developing new methods of plowing, fertilizing, and rotating crops.

Ruffin also believed in slavery. He felt slaves were an essential part of America's prosperity. Ruffin wrote a book to explain his beliefs, called *Slavery and Free Labor Described and Compared*. But his words could not convince those who were against slavery. Ruffin had only one response to their arguments—independence. The South had to leave the Union to survive.

On December 17, 1860, he attended a South Carolina convention to debate the issue of secession. When state legislators voted to secede, Ruffin was overjoyed; his nation was going to war at last. President Lincoln, however, declared that if there was to be a war, the Union would not fire the first shot. Edmund Ruffin decided the honor would have to be his.

On April 9, 1861, he traveled to Morris Island in Charleston Harbor, South Carolina. Ruffin knew that Union troops were trapped in Fort Sumter, just across the water, awaiting supplies and Federal reinforcements. Although he was 67 years old,

Ruffin convinced the guards to appoint him an honorary confederate private. Three days later he was allowed to man one of the Morris Island cannons. He aimed the barrel at Fort Sumter and at 4:30 in the morning, he fired the first shot of the Civil War.

Four years later, after more than a million casualties, when the Confederacy had surrendered and slavery was abolished, Ruffin placed a pistol to his own head and pulled the trigger. Some believe that Ruffin thought if the Confederacy could not exist, then neither should he.

STRANGE BEGINNINGS

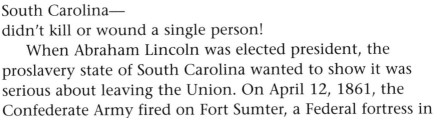

The Civil War was America's deadliest war. But, strangely enough, the battle that began the war—the bombardment of Fort Sumter, South Carolina— didn't kill or wound a single person!

When Abraham Lincoln was elected president, the proslavery state of South Carolina wanted to show it was serious about leaving the Union. On April 12, 1861, the Confederate Army fired on Fort Sumter, a Federal fortress in Charleston Harbor (in South Carolina). President Lincoln ordered the fort's commander, Major Robert Anderson, to fight back and hold his ground.

For 34 hours 4,000 artillery shells were fired back and forth between the two armies. Incredibly, no one was killed or injured in the exchange.

Finally, after two days of battle, Major Anderson was forced to surrender. He had run out of supplies and ammunition.

THE BATTLES

Want to be an instant
Civil War expert? Here's a
brief account of the Civil
War's major battles, who
won (or lost), and how each battle impacted the war.
The flags denote the winners of the battles.

Attack on Fort Sumter, South Carolina

April 12–13, 1861—Confederate Rebels fire the first shots of the
Civil War on Fort Sumter, in Charleston Harbor, South Carolina.
Union major Robert Anderson surrenders the fort after two days
of bombardment. **Casualties:** no injuries or deaths.

Battle of First Bull Run (First Manassas)

July 21, 1861—The first major land battle of the war takes
place at Bull Run, Virginia. 30,000 Union troops under
General Irvin McDowell are defeated by 32,000 Confederate
soldiers under Generals P.G.T. Beauregard and Joseph E.
Johnston. Local citizens bring picnic lunches and watch the
battle, thinking that the war will end in one day's fighting.
Casualties: 2,900 Union, 2,000 Confederate.

Battle of Ball's Bluff

October 21, 1861—1,700 Union troops cross the
Potomac River at Ball's Bluff, Virginia, and are driven
back by Confederate soldiers. **Casualties:** 347 Union,
153 Confederate.

Battle of the *Monitor* and the *Merrimac*

March 9, 1862—The first battle between iron warships takes
place at Hampton Roads, Virginia. The Union's *Monitor* and
Confederacy's *Merrimac* exchange cannon fire for four hours,
but neither ship is seriously damaged. **Casualties:** few injuries
and no deaths.

CIVIL WAR WORDS

Offensive: In military terms, being on the attack or threatening to attack.

The Peninsular Campaign

April 4–May 5, 1862—The first major *offensive* by Union general George B. McClellan's Army of the Potomac. 105,000 Union troops invade the Virginia Peninsula (the land between the York and James rivers), where they are met by 90,000 Confederates, commanded by Generals J.E. Johnston and Robert E. Lee. The Union captures Yorkstown and Williamsburg. **Casualties:** 16,000 Union, 20,000 Confederate.

Battle of Shiloh

April 6–7, 1862—Confederate forces attempt to block Union troops moving along the Tennessee River. Generals P.G.T. Beauregard and Albert Sidney Johnston command 40,000 Rebels, who meet a superior force of 63,000 Yankees under Generals Ulysses S. Grant and Don Carlos Buell. The Union defeats the Confederacy, and Confederate general Johnston is killed. **Casualties:** 12,000 Union, 10,000 Confederate.

Seven Days' Battle

June 25–July 2, 1862—Over the course of several battles, Confederate general Robert E. Lee halts General George B. McClellan's drive toward Richmond, Virginia, saving the Confederate capital from capture. Union troops are forced to retreat, but Confederate losses are heavy. **Casualties:** 16,000 Union, 20,000 Confederate.

Battle of Second Bull Run (Second Manassas)

August 29–30, 1862—Union general John Pope leads 75,000 soldiers against Confederate general Thomas "Stonewall" Jackson's 55,000 rebels at Bull Run, Virginia. The Confederates force the Yankees to retreat back to Washington, D.C., repeating their victory at First Bull Run the year before. **Casualties:** 16,000 Union, 9,500 Confederate.

Battle of Antietam

September 17, 1862—Confederate general Robert E. Lee leads a force of 40,000 soldiers against General McClellan's 90,000-man Union Army at Antietam, Maryland. The two armies fight the bloodiest single day's battle of the Civil War. Lee halts his invasion of the North and retreats to Virginia. **Casualties:** 12,000 Union, 10,000 Confederate.

Battle of Perryville

October 8, 1862—Confederate general Braxton Bragg attempts a second invasion of the North at Perryville, Kentucky. His 16,000 Rebel troops are outmatched by Union general Don Carlos Buell's army of 37,000. The Confederates are forced to retreat. **Casualties:** 4,200 Union, 3,400 Confederate.

Battle of Fredericksburg

December 13, 1862—Union general Ambrose Burnside leads a huge army of 106,000 Federal soldiers into Fredericksburg, Virginia, to attack Robert E. Lee's Confederate Army. Lee's 72,500 rebels defend their position and the Union is forced to retreat, suffering great losses. **Casualties:** 12,000 Union, 5,000 Confederate.

Battle of Murfreesboro

December 31, 1862–January 3, 1863—At Murfreesboro, Tennessee, Confederate general Braxton Bragg's 38,000 troops are attacked by Union general William Rosecrans's force of 47,000 men. Three days of bloody fighting lead nowhere and both armies withdraw. **Casualties:** 12,000 Union, 12,000 Confederate.

Battle of Chancellorsville

May 1–4, 1863—Major General Joseph Hooker takes command of the Union's Army of the Potomac and attacks the Confederate Army at Chancellorsville, Virginia. Even though they are outnumbered, 60,000 Confederate troops force Hooker's 113,000 Yankee soldiers to retreat. Confederate general Thomas "Stonewall" Jackson is accidentally shot by his own troops during the battle. He dies shortly after. **Casualties:** 17,000 Union, 13,000 Confederate.

Battle of Vicksburg

May 22–July 4, 1863—Union general Ulysses S. Grant attempts to invade Vicksburg, Mississippi, which is well defended by the Confederates. Despite repeated attacks, his 33,000-man army can gain no ground on Vicksburg's 37,000 defenders. Grant blockades the city and forces its inhabitants to surrender or starve. The Union then gains control of the entire Mississippi River, dividing the Confederacy in half. Ulysses S. Grant earns his famous nickname Unconditional Surrender, because he refuses to make peace until the battle is won. **Casualties:** 9,300 Union, 10,000 Confederate.

Battle of Gettysburg

July 1–3, 1863—Confederate general Robert E. Lee attempts another invasion of the North at Gettysburg, Pennsylvania. For three days his 75,000 Rebel troops battle General George Meade's 88,000 Union defenders, but they are forced to retreat to Virginia again. It is the bloodiest battle of the Civil War and the beginning of the Union's drive toward victory. On November 19, 1863, President Lincoln delivers his famous Gettysburg Address, dedicating the battlefield to the Union soldiers who died there. **Casualties:** 23,000 Union, 28,000 Confederate.

Battle of Chickamauga

September 19–20, 1863—Confederate general Braxton Bragg attacks Union General William Rosecrans's army at Chickamauga Creek, Georgia. The Union army is forced to retreat to Chattanooga, Tennessee, 15 miles away. The Confederacy wins the battle but suffers heavy casualties. The

Southern Army's numbers dwindle. **Casualties:** 16,000 Union, 18,000 Confederate.

Battle of Chattanooga

November 23–25, 1863—Confederate general Braxton Bragg attacks General Grant's forces at Chattanooga, Tennessee. The Union's 60,000 soldiers defeat the Confederacy's 40,000 invaders, forcing them to retreat to Georgia. The Union gains control of Southern railways, making it difficult for the Confederacy to supply its troops with food and ammunition. **Casualties:** 6,000 Union, 6,700 Confederate.

Battle of the Wilderness

May 5–6, 1864—General U.S. Grant leads a huge army of 119,000 Union soldiers toward Richmond, Virginia, the Confederate capital. They are met by General Robert E. Lee's 65,000 defenders in a forest outside the city. The two armies battle for two days, and many soldiers die as the result of smoke inhalation from fires burning in the woods. Neither side gains any ground, but Grant decides to detour and continue his invasion rather than retreat. **Casualties:** 15,000 Union, 8,000 Confederate.

Battle of Spotsylvania Court House

May 8–12, 1864—Grant's 104,000-man army pushes toward Richmond, attacking 53,000 Confederate defenders at Spotsylvania Court House, Virginia. After five days of heavy fighting, neither side gains ground, and the battle ends in a stalemate. Grant is forced to halt and make new plans. Lee's army, however, is exhausted. **Casualties:** 17,000 Union, 9,000 Confederate.

Battle of Cold Harbor

June 1–3, 1864—Grant continues to wear down the Confederate Army, leading a 108,000-man force against Lee's

59,000 Rebels at Cold Harbor, Virginia, just a few miles outside Richmond. Although many Union soldiers are killed, Grant's huge army is able to bypass the weakening Rebels and invade Richmond, the Confederate capital. **Casualties:** 12,000 Union, 1,500 Confederate.

Battle of Franklin

November 30, 1864—Confederate general John Bell Hood leads a 27,000-man assault on the Union Army at Franklin, Tennessee. The campaign is a disaster and six Confederate generals are killed in the fighting. **Casualties:** 1,200 Union, 5,500 Confederate.

Battle of Nashville

December 15–17, 1864—Union general George Thomas commands 50,000 troops in an attack on General Hood's 23,000-man army at Nashville, Tennessee, the state capital. The Union forces the Confederacy to flee, leading to Tennessee's restoration to the Union. It is one of the last large battles of the Civil War. **Casualties:** 3,000 Union, 6,400 Confederate.

Battle of Sayler's Creek

April 6, 1865—The Union's Army of the Potomac attacks the Confederacy's Army of Northern Virginia at Sayler's Creek, Virginia, and destroys their remaining supply trains. This battle strikes the final blow to the retreating Confederacy as they make their way toward Appomattox Court House, Virginia. There, Confederate general Robert E. Lee surrenders the Rebel Army and ends the war on April 9. **Casualties:** 2,400 Union, 8,000 Confederate.

A SOLDIER'S LIFE
"The Terrors of This Battle"

"I cannot give you an idea of the terrors of this battle. I believe it was as hard a contested battle as was ever fought on the American continent, or perhaps anywhere else . . . for ten long hours . . . the firing did not cease for a moment. Try to picture . . . 100,000 men, all loading and firing as fast as they could."

—Confederate private J.W. Reid,
4th Regiment, South Carolina Volunteers
(excerpted from *War, Terrible War* by Joy Hakim)

DIARY

THE CIVIL WAR GOES TO EUROPE

One of the Civil War's most unusual sea battles wasn't fought along the American coastline but across the Atlantic Ocean— in Europe!

On June 11, 1864, the Confederate steamship *Alabama*, which had been built by the British to aid the South (England imported cotton and other plantation goods from the South before the war), sailed into port at Cherbourg, France, to replenish supplies. This ship had sunk 68 Union vessels, and many Yankee prisoners were being held on board. Just then, the Union warship *Kearsarge* appeared in the harbor. The *Kearsarge*'s captain, John A. Winslow, insisted the *Alabama* hand over its prisoners. The *Alabama*'s captain, Raphael Semmes, refused.

The two ships began to fire at each other as French citizens watched and cheered from the shore. A famous French painter, Édouard Manet, even sketched a picture of the scene. After an hour and a half of cannon fire, the *Alabama* began to sink. Its crew abandoned ship, and the Yankee prisoners were set free.

A SOLDIER'S LIFE
"I Thought My Head Was Gone"

"June 1864. An order came for a report to be sent to brigade Head-quarters and I sat down to write it out.

"Several of the enemy's batteries had then opened fire, but as we were a little under the hill, I thought we were in no great danger from the shells, which were flying over—in fact we had gotten so used to the shells that we scarcely noticed them.

"I was only a few minutes writing the report, and raised my head to ask the Colonel if I should sign his name to the paper, and had bent over and had about finished signing the paper, when suddenly every thing got dark, and I became unconscious.

"If I had been sitting erect, when the fragment of shell struck me, I never would have known what hurt me. When I came to my senses . . . I could not imagine, at first, what was the matter; the first thought that entered my mind was that my head was gone and I put my hand up to ascertain whether it was still on my shoulders."

—Confederate private John S. Jackman,
The Orphan Brigade, 1st Regiment, Kentucky
(excerpted from *Diary of a Confederate Soldier*
by William C. Davis)

THE MAN WHOSE HOUSE BEGAN AND ENDED THE CIVIL WAR

Amazingly enough, the Civil War began and ended at houses owned by the same man, a Virginian named Wilmer McLean.

McLean was a grocer with a home at Bull Run—called Manassas in the South—which was a railway center near Washington, D.C. (Southerners often had different names for places than Northerners.) On July 21, 1861, Confederate general P.G.T. Beauregard used McLean's house as a temporary headquarters. While he was there, Yankee soldiers attacked. A cannonball came crashing through one wall, completely destroying McLean's kitchen. A year later, a second battle (called Second Bull Run or Second Manassas) at the same site convinced McLean to move to a quieter area.

McLean found a brick farmhouse in an out-of-the-way Virginian town called Appomattox Court House. On April 9, 1865, Confederate general Robert E. Lee chose McLean's house as an appropriate site to surrender his army to Union General Ulysses S. Grant.

Lee signed surrender papers in McLean's front parlor, ending the Civil War. But the war was not over for Wilmer McLean. Eager souvenir hounds grabbed everything they could from the historic site. They even broke dishes and ripped the furniture to shreds.

THE SOLDIERS

The Civil War was fought by soldiers of every possible age, race, and description. There were black soldiers, Indian soldiers, cowboy soldiers. There were soldiers in their 80s who had fought many wars, and runaway volunteers who were only 9 years old. There were even soldiers who came from overseas to join in the fight. When the fighting began, however, it didn't matter what a soldier's background was, where he was from, or how old he was. Most often, Northern soldiers were just called Billy Yank and Southern soldiers Johnny Reb.

WHAT'S YOUR REGIMENT?

In both the Union and the Confederacy, army *regiments* were often formed by the citizens of individual towns or areas. Usually, a regiment's soldiers all had something in common with one another. These soldiers gave their regiments

CIVIL WAR WORDS

Regiment: A military group of three battalions, commanded by a colonel. A regiment forms the basic unit of an army division.

distinctive nicknames, and it was by these nicknames that they generally were remembered.

The Union's 13th Pennsylvania Reserve Regiment, for example, was called the Pennsylvania Bucktails because its members were lumberjacks and woodsmen. They often displayed their hunting skills by wearing a bucktail (a deer's tail) on their Union Army caps.

The Union's 100th Indiana Regiment was known as the Persimmon Regiment because its members loved persimmons so much that they would stop fighting whenever they found a persimmon tree and climb into its branches to pick some fruit.

Sometimes soldiers' professions before the war gave regiments their nicknames. The 89th Illinois was called the Railroad Regiment because it consisted of former railroad employees. A Confederate brigade formed by Robert G. Touchman, a Polish soldier before the war, soon became known as the Louisiana Polish Brigade. The 33rd Illinois was dubbed the Teachers' Regiment because most of its members were either teachers or students before enlisting in the army.

The Union's 37th Iowa was dubbed the Graybeard Regiment because all of its soldiers were 45 years of age or older (twice as old as most Civil War combatants). Some of its soldiers were in their 80s. Even their drummer "boy," Nicholas Ramey, was 72 years old!

★★★★ OLD ABE, THE SOLDIER'S MASCOT ★★★★

There was one Union Army member who had an aerial view of every battle—Old Abe, the eagle.

When the war began, a soldier in the 8th Wisconsin Regiment traded an Indian five bushels of corn for the eagle and named him Old Abe, after President Lincoln. The bird was soon a constant companion, following his master everywhere.

During battle, Old Abe would fly high above the scene, returning after the firing had stopped. Like many Civil War veterans, he was shot during battle, but Old Abe survived and lived for 15 years after the war.

Today his stuffed remains can be seen on display at the Wisconsin State Museum.

★ ★

SOLDIERS WITHOUT A HOME

One of the most famous fighting units in the Confederate Army was the 1st Kentucky Brigade. Its soldiers had a reputation for hard fighting. Their true fame, however, came from the fact that they were soldiers without a home. They were known as the Orphan Brigade.

When the Civil War broke out, Kentucky's citizens were divided in their sympathies for North and South. After all, both Abraham Lincoln and Jefferson Davis were Kentucky natives. Some citizens formed regiments that enlisted in the Union Army. Others, such as the 1st Kentucky Brigade, headed south to fight for the Confederacy.

Within a year after the war began, Union forces controlled Kentucky territory, and those who had sided with the Confederacy could no longer return home. The 1st Kentucky Brigade's commander was Major General John C. Breckinridge. He looked at his men and called them "poor orphans." The name stuck, and the unit became known as the Orphan Brigade.

The Orphan Brigade fought in many important battles and was sent wherever the fighting was hardest. Over time, as the war raged on, most of the orphan soldiers were killed. By the last year of the war, there were no longer enough of them to form a complete fighting unit.

At war's end, those in the Orphan Brigade who had survived were finally able to return home to their beloved state of Kentucky. They were orphans no longer.

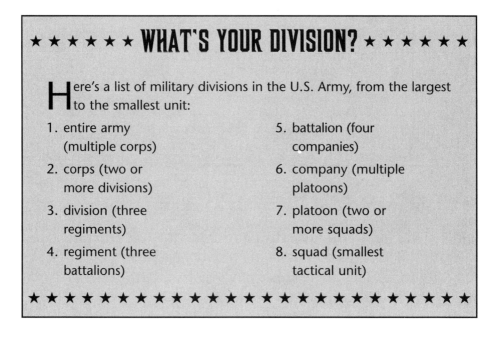

★ ★ ★ ★ ★ ★ WHAT'S YOUR DIVISION? ★ ★ ★ ★ ★ ★

Here's a list of military divisions in the U.S. Army, from the largest to the smallest unit:

1. entire army (multiple corps)
2. corps (two or more divisions)
3. division (three regiments)
4. regiment (three battalions)
5. battalion (four companies)
6. company (multiple platoons)
7. platoon (two or more squads)
8. squad (smallest tactical unit)

★ ★

BLACKS JOIN IN THE FIGHT

After President Lincoln issued his *Emancipation* Proclamation on January 1, 1863, slaves in the South were declared free. Since the Confederate states considered themselves a separate nation, however, the Emancipation Proclamation was ignored by slave owners and had no legal impact in the South. But slaves did hear about President Lincoln's proclamation. They knew that if the Union won the war, they would be free.

Northern blacks, who already were free, were now allowed to enlist in the Union Army. Though, the risks for black soldiers were greater than for white soldiers. If caught by the Confederacy, blacks might have been sold into slavery or killed, instead of detained as prisoners of war.

Still, many black people realized that fighting in the army could help their struggle for equal rights. "Once let the black man get upon his person the brass letters *U.S.*; let him get an eagle on his button and a musket on his shoulder and bullets in his pocket," proclaimed black abolitionist Frederick Douglass, an ex-slave, "and there is no power on earth which can deny that he has earned the right to citizenship in the United States."

CIVIL WAR WORDS

Emancipation: Freeing from imprisonment or slavery. Union president Abraham Lincoln issued the Emancipation Proclamation to declare that all slaves living in the Confederate states were free after January 1, 1863. The Confederate government, however, refused to accept the Emancipation Proclamation and Southern slaves were not freed until after the war was over, on April 9, 1865.

Douglass's mission to recruit black regiments for the Northern war effort was aided by two other black leaders—John Mercer Langston, a self-taught lawyer from Virginia, and Martin Robinson Delany, a self-trained physician. Together, the three men spoke to free blacks throughout the Union, urging them to help free their captive brethren in the South.

FROM SLAVES TO SOLDIERS

When Northern blacks joined the Union Army, white Yankee soldiers were uncertain how to treat them. Black soldiers had never fought alongside white soldiers as equals before. In the beginning, most blacks were given camp chores and not allowed to shoulder a gun in battle.

Then, in July 1863, an all-black regiment called the 54th

Massachusetts, commanded by a white officer, Colonel Robert Gould Shaw, was assigned to attack Fort Wagner in Charleston Harbor, South Carolina. It was a dangerous mission, but the 54th Massachusetts fought so bravely that no one could question whether black soldiers were the equals of white soldiers anymore.

Even the Confederates realized something had changed. "The day you make soldiers of [slaves] is the beginning of the end of the revolution," said Major General Howell Cobb. "And if slaves seem good soldiers, then our whole theory of slavery is wrong."

INDIAN SOLDIERS

Both the Union and Confederacy convinced Indian warriors to join in the fight, forming regiments named after tribes, such as the 1st Cherokee Mounted Rifles. Although they were appreciated as ferocious fighters, the Indians had a reputation for scalping fallen soldiers. They also had no real loyalty to either the North or the South, since both sides were fighting over land that had once belonged to the Indians. Because of this, many Indian soldiers switched sides whenever it suited them. In fact, very often, Union and Confederate generals recruited Indians simply to fight against other Indians.

There were some Indians who played important roles in the course of the Civil War. A Cherokee chief named Stand Watie became a Confederate brigadier general, commanding an all-Indian brigade in Mississippi. He was a fierce fighter and, at war's end, was the last Confederate general to lay down his arms and give up the fight.

A Seneca Indian named Ely Parker became a brigadier general for the Union. He was so trustworthy that General Ulysses S. Grant appointed him as his personal secretary. When Confederate general Lee surrendered to Grant at Appomattox Court House on April 9, 1865, it was Parker who wrote down the terms of the agreement.

WHEN BOYS WENT TO WAR

In addition to its many other names (see p. 9), the Civil War was often referred to as The Boy's War, because so many soldiers were such young boys.

On the Union side, statistics show that more than 2,000,000 soldiers—three quarters of the entire army—were 21 years old and younger. Half of those were 18 and younger; about 200,000 soldiers were 16 and younger; 100,000 were 15 and under; 300 soldiers were 13 and under. In addition, there were at least 25 Union Army soldiers who were only 10 years old and younger! Confederate statistics show a similar percentage of young soldiers.

Many of the youngest soldiers joined the army as members of the Fife and Drummers Corps, playing music as the soldiers marched into battle. Sometimes, however, they would drop their instruments and pick up guns to join in the fighting themselves.

Even some of the Civil War's commanders were quite young. Union *brevet* major general Galusha Pennypacker was only 17 when the war began, younger than some of the soldiers he commanded.

CIVIL WAR WORDS

Brevet: A higher rank than what the soldier is getting paid for.

JOHNNY CLEM, DRUMMER BOY

One of the most famous members of the Fife and Drummers Corps was Johnny Clem, who ran away from home and joined the 22nd Michigan Regiment when he was only 9 years old.

A SOLDIER'S LIFE

"They Said I Could Hold a Drum"

"I wanted to fight the Rebs, but I was very small and they would not give me a musket. The next day I went back and the man behind the desk said I looked as if I could hold a drum and if I wanted I could join that way. I did, but I was not happy to change a musket for a stick."

—journal entry,
Union drummer boy, age 12
(excerpted from *The Boy's War* by Jim Murphy)

Clem's sister said, "He was an expert drummer and soon made his way into the affections of officers and soldiers."

Like many drummer boys, Clem dreamed of being a real Union soldier and fighting in battle. But instead, he helped with camp chores, cleaning the dishes and tending to the horses. During battle he drummed to help keep the troops in line (the sound helped the soldiers stay grouped together). Like all drummer boys, Clem also relayed commands over the sound of gunfire with special drumming signals.

Then, during the Battle of Shiloh (April 6–7, 1862), a cannonball exploded off a tree and destroyed Johnny Clem's drum. With nothing else to do, he picked up a gun and started shooting at the Confederate soldiers. After winning the battle, his fellow soldiers took to calling him Johnny Shiloh. Johnny Clem had become a real soldier after all.

The regiment gave Clem a special musket, adapted for his small size. At the Battle of Chickamauga (September 19–20, 1863), he faced a Confederate cavalryman who charged him on horseback, shouting "Surrender, you little Yankee devil!" Clem fired his musket and knocked the Rebel from his horse. Afterward, he was promoted to sergeant and decorated for his bravery—even though he was only 11 years old!

At the end of the war, Johnny Clem was promoted to lieutenant. He remained in the army until 1915, when he finally retired, a 63-year-old major general. Until then, the little drummer boy had been the last living Civil War veteran still serving in America's armed forces.

THE INJURED SOLDIERS' SERVICE

Just because a man was disabled or unable to join a fighting regiment didn't mean he couldn't serve in the army. A special corps of soldiers, called the Invalid Corps, was formed to protect the area surrounding Washington, D.C., the Union capital. Later, as the Invalid Corps became filled with soldiers who were injured battle veterans, its name was changed to the Veteran Reserve Corps (VRC).

Service in the VRC was considered light duty because military leaders didn't believe Confederate soldiers could get close enough to attack the area. Each member of the Veteran Reserve Corps was allowed to serve according to his ability. VRC soldiers who were sickly but uninjured were issued rifles. Those with just one arm were given lightweight pistols or swords. Those unable to carry any weapon were trained as nurses.

Then, on July 11, 1864, Confederate general Jubal Early decided to attack the lightly defended capital. "We were all in high spirits and felt that we were about to enter the city with little or no opposition," said Isaac Bradwell, a private under Early's command. "We would drag 'old Abe' [President Abraham Lincoln] out of hiding and carry him in triumph off with us as a trophy to show our comrades."

As Early's Rebels began to march on Fort Stevens, the outermost Washington, D.C., defense post, the Union scrambled for soldiers to repel the attack. The Veteran Reserve Corps was pressed into active duty, and bravely battled the invaders until non-VRC reinforcements could arrive.

President Lincoln, instead of "hiding," as the Confederates said, rode a carriage to witness the fighting himself. As the president watched, some of the Union's bravest soldiers rose above their disabilities and helped drive the Rebels back into Virginia.

A SOLDIER'S LIFE

"This Boy Puts You All to Shame"

"A cannonball came bouncing across the cornfield, kicking up dirt and dust each time it struck the earth. Many of the men in our company took shelter behind a stone wall, but I stood where I was and never stopped drumming. An officer came by on horseback and chastised the men, saying 'this boy puts you all to shame. Get up and move forward.' We all began moving across the cornfield . . . even when the fighting was at its fiercest and I was frightened, I stood straight and did as I was ordered."

DIARY

—journal entry,
Union drummer boy
(excerpted from *The Boy's War* by Jim Murphy)

CAMP LIFE

When the Civil War began, most of the soldiers in both the Union and the Confederacy were unaccustomed to the hardships of war. They pictured battle in heroic terms, imagining themselves charging against the enemy and returning home as heroes within a day or two.

As the war dragged on and the days turned into weeks, months, and years, soldiers found there were often long waiting periods between battles. They didn't return home after fighting, but instead lived in camps, waiting for the next battle orders.

Life in Civil War camps was very difficult. There were never enough tents for everybody to use. Soldiers fortunate enough to be near woods could cut down trees and build cabins for shelter. Others, stuck out in open country, had to dig holes in the ground to escape the heat and cold.

CIVIL WAR WORDS

Outfit: In the military, a single group or squad of soldiers.

There was not much to do to pass the time between battles. Some *outfits* marched in formation or practiced their marksmanship. Most soldiers, however, spent hours writing letters home each day. They read and discussed any news from the outside world, washed and mended their clothes, and played cards together. Some soldiers even staged flea and lice races, betting heavily on the vermin picked off their own bodies! In winter, troops staged mock battles, substituting snowballs for musket balls.

But as the war continued, and more and more soldiers faced the horrors of combat, recruits came to realize that camp life was actually a pleasant, peaceful time. It may have been slow and uneventful, but at least it was a chance to live another day.

A SOLDIER'S LIFE

"It Appears to Be Fine Exercise"

"The prisoners nearly every evening are engaged in a game they call 'base-ball,' which notwithstanding the heat they prosecute with persevering energy. I don't understand the game, as there is a great deal of running and little apparent gain, but those who play it get very excited over it, and it appears to be fine exercise."

—journal entry,
Confederate prisoner John Delhaney
(excerpted from *The Boy's War* by Jim Murphy)

THE DIARY THAT SAVED A LIFE

Soldiers who carried a regiment's battle flag were an easy target for enemy riflemen. They carried flags, not guns, and so were often among the first killed in battle. When Union sergeant Francis M. McMillen, flag bearer for the 110th Ohio Regiment, was shot squarely in the chest, however, he found his life miraculously saved—by his own diary!

The day was March 25, 1865, and McMillen's troop was attacking Confederate forces at Fort Fisher, Virginia. Just as gunfire erupted, McMillen was struck by a bullet aimed straight at his heart. Fortunately, McMillen always carried his diary in his breast pocket, using it to record his wartime experiences. The bullet struck the leather diary, ricocheted off, smashed his pocket watch, and then lodged itself in his brass belt buckle. McMillen was unharmed and lived to write about his good fortune—in the diary itself!

THE WAGON THAT WENT TO WAR

Among the most important weapons a Civil War army brigade had were its supply wagons, which carried food and other important materials behind the marching troops. When they didn't have supply wagons, soldiers were forced to pick fruit from the trees, or even beg and steal for food.

There were two Civil War generals famous for marching their troops over vast distances very quickly, Union general Sherman and Confederate general "Stonewall" Jackson. Both leaders relied on supply wagons to feed their troops while on the move.

General Sherman's army used a caravan of 2,500 supply wagons on his victorious march from Philadelphia,

★ ★ ★ ★ ★ ★ ★ ★ ★ ★ ★

THE 900-POUND BULLET

The guns used by both Union and Confederate troops were so hard to aim accurately that soldiers missed far more often than they hit their targets. One Union military expert estimated that for each Confederate soldier shot, 240 pounds of gunpowder and 900 pounds of lead were used!

★ ★ ★ ★ ★ ★ ★ ★ ★ ★ ★

Pennsylvania, to Atlanta, Georgia. Though many of the wagons broke down or were destroyed along the way, one wagon survived every battle from the start of the war to the finish.

Throughout this wagon's many years of service, soldiers wrote its battle history on the wooden side panels. They also added up how many miles the wagon had covered—4,160, more than enough to travel across the entire country!

At the war's end, the sturdy little wagon was given a hero's welcome. It was paraded in Washington, D.C., with the rest of the Union troops and given a final resting place in the nation's capital city for many years longer.

TRADING WITH THE ENEMY

Wherever Union and Confederate soldiers met on the battlefield, they fought to the death. In between battles, however, they often traded supplies with each other, acting more like business partners than fighting enemies.

When Union general Ambrose Burnside massed his troops opposite Confederate general Lee's soldiers at the Rappahannock River in Virginia in December of 1862, both armies were prepared for fierce battle.

While waiting for orders to fight, the soldiers tried to equip themselves as best they could—even if that meant trading with the enemy across the river. Northern soldiers usually had plenty of sugar, coffee, and clothing, all of which were in short supply in the South. Confederate soldiers, on the other hand, had fine tobacco, which the Yankee troops loved to smoke.

The two sides set up a trading system. They strung a cable to carry items back and forth across the rocky gorge between their two armies. In addition, handmade rafts were floated from shore to shore. Soldiers included messages with their supply packages, requesting specific items they wanted in return.

This sort of collaboration with the enemy was illegal, but Union and Confederate officers usually allowed it before and in between battles. They knew their soldiers were happier

★ ★ ★ ★ ★ ★ ★ ★ ★ ★ ★ ★

ABE LINCOLN, CONFEDERATE SOLDIER

Two Abraham Lincolns actually served in the Civil War, one for the Union and one for the Confederacy! Company F in the 1st Virginia Cavalry listed among its troops a private named Abraham Lincoln. In 1864, however, the young soldier deserted and joined the Yankee forces, so by the end of the war, the North had *both* Abraham Lincolns fighting on its side.

★ ★ ★ ★ ★ ★ ★ ★ ★ ★ ★ ★

when well supplied, and it helped take the recruits' minds off the horrors of battle.

Eventually, of course, soldiers returned to the business of fighting. For Burnside's and Lee's troops at the Rappahannock River, five days of fighting turned 18,000 of the trading soldiers into casualties of war.

A SOLDIER'S LIFE
A Meal Time Break

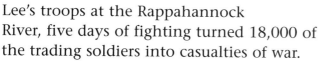

"There are blackberries in the field so our boys and the Yanks made a bargain not to fire at each other, and went out in the field, leaving one man on each post with the arms, and gathered berries together and talked over the fight, and traded tobacco and coffee and newspapers as peacefully and kindly as if they had not been engaged for seven days in butchering one another."

—journal entry,
Confederate soldier
(excerpted from *The Civil War* by Geoffrey C. Ward
with Ric Burns and Ken Burns)

WHEN MUSIC WAS MIGHTIER THAN THE MUSKET

Both Union and Confederate armies had musicians who traveled with the soldiers, entertaining them between battles to help relieve the agony of war. Sometimes these musicians became so popular that soldiers preferred to lay down their arms and listen to music rather than continue the fighting.

During one three-day battle in Atlanta, Georgia, a cornet (a kind of trumpet) player from Confederate major Arthur Shoaff's battalion walked up and down the line, playing for the Rebel troops. One day the fighting was particularly heavy and the cornet player didn't appear.

Through the battle smoke a Union soldier shouted, "Hey, Johnny [Reb]! We want that cornet player."

The Confederate soldiers shouted back, "He would play, but he's afraid you'll spoil his horn."

"We'll hold fire."

"All right, Yanks."

The cornet player then appeared and began to play, drawing applause and cheers from both Union and Confederate troops.

After the music ended, both armies continued their fighting.

PRESIDENT LINCOLN AIDS A REBEL

To many Northerners, the Confederates were traitors of the worst kind. As Rebels, they deserved to be punished or executed. President Lincoln, however, believed that a little kindness could go a long way toward reuniting the nation once the war was over. One day the president went so far as to grant a favor to one of his fiercest enemies—a Confederate general.

It was April 3, 1865. Confederate general Robert E. Lee called his remaining forces to Amelia Court House, Virginia, for a last, desperate battle against the invading Yankee Army. Confederate brigadier general Rufus Barringer rushed his troops toward the scene. On the way, Barringer's men were caught in an ambush by Union forces. Barringer was taken prisoner and brought to Federal headquarters for questioning. President Lincoln happened to be touring the facility and, upon hearing of Barringer's capture, asked to meet the Rebel leader.

Lincoln greeted the prisoner kindly and said, "There was a Barringer in Congress with me."

The general nodded. "That was my brother, sir."

Lincoln and Barringer talked about earlier days, before the war. Lincoln felt sympathy for his captured foe. "Do you think I could be of any service to you?" he asked.

General Barringer was surprised by the question. "If anyone could be of service to a poor devil in my situation," he said, "I presume you are the man."

Lincoln wrote a brief note to his secretary of war, Edwin Stanton, and asked that Barringer be made "as comfortable as possible under the circumstances."

But the Confederate general's luck had ended. Six days later the war was over, and shortly thereafter, President Lincoln was assassinated. Barringer, because of his unusual meeting with the president, was suspected of being involved in the murder. Instead of being treated with kindness, Barringer was held under close guard for three more months—long after nearly all other Rebel prisoners had been freed.

SPIES & SECRET ALLIES

When a country goes to war, soldiers aren't the only ones engaged in the fight. In both the Union and the Confederacy, every citizen was expected to do his or her part to help. Every man, woman, and child could have been an enemy spy or a secret ally. Agents of war were everywhere.

THE UNION'S BEST SPY

One of the Union's best spies was a former detective named Timothy Webster, a brilliant actor and master of disguise.

His spying started soon after the Civil War began. The government sent Webster to observe Confederate troops in Kentucky and Tennessee, where he pretended to be a local citizen who hated the North. When somebody recognized Webster as a Washington, D.C., detective, he called his accuser a liar and knocked him flat to the ground. The ruse worked, and Webster was championed as a great fighter for the Southern cause.

He was asked to join the Knights of Liberty, a group of Rebels planning an attack on the Union capital. Webster eagerly agreed. He secretly passed the Knights' plans on to Union headquarters in Washington, D.C., and Federal agents burst into a Knights meeting and arrested the entire group of plotters. On the way to prison at Fort McHenry, Webster was allowed to escape. To the rest of the Knights of Liberty, this only made him more of a legend.

Webster's Confederate disguise was so believable, in fact, that a young Federal agent arrested him, thinking he had captured a Southern spy. After being taken to prison, his true identity was revealed and Webster was released (or rather, he was allowed to "escape" while being transferred back to Fort McHenry). His reputation as "uncatchable" spread throughout the South. The Confederate government was so impressed with his abilities that it granted Webster a pass allowing free travel throughout the Confederacy.

Then disaster struck. Webster fell ill with rheumatism, a painful muscle disorder. He was forced to lie low in a hotel until his condition improved. Federal officials, however, grew worried when they didn't hear from him as usual. Two inexperienced spies were sent South to hunt for him. They were soon caught by Confederate agents and sentenced to hang.

One of the spies panicked and tried to gain his freedom by revealing Webster's true identity. The Confederates, of course, immediately arrested Webster and sentenced him to hang, too. He was executed on April 29, 1862, a true Union hero.

THE FIRST LADY . . . A CONFEDERATE SPY?

When the Civil War broke out, many families were divided in their loyalty to the Northern or Southern cause. Even Mary Todd Lincoln, the Union's first lady, found her brother and three brothers-in-law fighting for the Confederacy.

Because she was married to President Lincoln, this became a source of great suspicion among Northerners. Some people claimed the First Lady was "two thirds proslavery and the other third secesh [secessionist]." Whenever Mrs. Lincoln wrote letters to her family, people suspected she might be passing on vital wartime information. Some whispered that the first lady was, in fact, working as a Confederate spy.

A secret Senate committee gathered to discuss Mrs. Lincoln's loyalties. Soon after the meeting began, the door to their chamber opened, and there stood the president himself. With sadness in his eyes, Lincoln said, "I, Abraham Lincoln, President of the United States, appear of my own volition before this committee of the Senate to say that, I, of my own knowledge, know that it is untrue that any of my family hold treasonable communication with the enemy."

The senators came to their senses, and no further discussion was made of Mrs. Lincoln's wartime activities.

THE GREAT TRAIN ROBBERY

On April 12, 1862, the Civil War was exactly a year old. To soldiers who hadn't seen much fighting yet, it was still something of a grand adventure. And so it was for 23 Union soldiers of the 33rd Ohio Infantry who volunteered for one of the war's

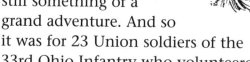

boldest missions—stealing the Confederate locomotive the *General* from the Rebel Army itself.

Railroads were an important part of the war campaign, supplying troops, carrying weapons, and evacuating wounded soldiers. The Union had an advantage over the South: There were twice as many miles of railway in Northern territory. Stealing a Confederate train and destroying Rebel rail lines could make a big difference in the North's ability to crush the Southern war effort.

Disguised as civilians, the 23 volunteers followed a simple plan. Sneaking south to Chattanooga, Tennessee, in small groups, they told all who asked that they were Kentucky citizens who hated the Yankees and wanted to enlist in the Rebel cause. They boarded a train that was heading south to Atlanta, Georgia, and then the Yankees seized control of another Confederate locomotive called the *General.*

The surprised Confederates watched in amazement as the train headed the wrong way—back toward Chattanooga. As they passed each station, the Yankee soldiers slowed down to cut telegraph lines, so that news of their theft couldn't be relayed to a station ahead.

Behind the fleeing volunteers, however, was William Allen Fuller, the *General*'s conductor, who was determined not to let his train fall into enemy hands. Fuller used a railroad handcart to get himself to another train, then chased after the *General.* Halfway to Chattanooga, traveling at speeds up to 60 miles an hour, he caught up with the Yankees at last.

In desperation, the Yankee soldiers aboard the *General* uncoupled box cars and sent them hurtling backward down the track. Each time, Fuller would reverse his own train's direction, link up with the approaching boxcar, then change direction and resume the forward chase. Finally, the *General* ran out of steam and ground to a halt. The Ohio volunteers quickly fled into the surrounding woods. It was every man for himself.

Of the 23 men, only 2 succeeded in escaping capture. The others were tried and found guilty of spying. After the first eight men were hanged, eight of the remaining prisoners staged a daring prison escape and managed to make their way back to Union forces.

By March 1863, the rest of the train robbers were exchanged for Confederate prisoners and returned to the North. All the survivors of the great escapade were awarded the Congressional Medal of Honor. They were the first soldiers given this high honor. Their dangerous exploit had inspired Union soldiers everywhere to give their all in battling a determined enemy.

SUE MUNDY, THE OUTLAW WHO NEVER EXISTED . . . AND HANGED FOR IT!

High on the Union's wartime "most-wanted" list was a Confederate raider named Sue Mundy, who led a band of Rebels in Kentucky. She grew to fame in 1864, when the Louisville *Courier* featured regular reports of her exploits, stealing guns and other supplies for the Confederacy. But when the Union finally sent soldiers to arrest her . . . they discovered Sue Mundy didn't exist!

The *Courier* had invented the character of a daring female Rebel in order to sell more newspapers. The band of Confederate raiders described in the articles was actually led by a young man named Marcellus Clark, who was easily mistaken for a woman because of his long, flowing hair.

After the Union captured him, Marcellus (who came from a wealthy, distinguished family) insisted he be treated with the same respect due any other prisoner of war. But the Union didn't take kindly to the newspaper's trickery. Clark, alias Sue Mundy, was hanged just as the papers had described him—as a common outlaw.

A NATION OF RUNAWAY SPIES

Both the Union and the Confederacy used spies to learn of enemy encampments, troop movements, and other important wartime information. But spying on the enemy was difficult and dangerous, especially far behind enemy lines. Fortunately for the Union, there were many volunteers who knew every detail of Confederate defenses and were eager to help the Northern cause—escaped Southern slaves.

A slave needed a good understanding of Confederate troop whereabouts to avoid being captured while sneaking northward. Every soldier, every weapon, every important detail along the way, was memorized for safety's sake. Once behind Union lines, newly liberated slaves were more than happy to share what they had seen with Federal officers.

Because of this information, Union officers often had as detailed a knowledge of Rebel troop locations as their Confederate counterparts. It was an advantage that played a decisive role in the long war campaign.

A WAR BETWEEN THE INDIANS

When the Civil War erupted and Northern and Southern states began to choose sides, one territory remained neutral, joining neither the Union nor the Confederacy. This was Indian Territory, an area which would become the state of Oklahoma in 1907.

But it wasn't long before the Indian Territory's many tribes found themselves choosing sides in the white man's Civil War, after all. A month after the war began, Confederate general Albert Pike entered Indian Territory, hoping to forge a treaty with the *Five Civilized Tribes*—the Chickasaw, Choctaw, Cherokee, Creek, and Seminole Indians.

The Choctaw and Chickasaw, whose land was closest to Texas (a Confederate state), agreed to help the Rebels. But the Creek and Seminole Indians (whose land was closer to the free states of Kansas and Missouri), tended to side with the North.

68

John Ross, the chief of the Cherokees, was unsure whom to support. At first, he thought the Rebels would win the war and convinced his people to aid the South. After the Battle of Gettysburg, however, when Union soldiers began their conquest of the South, Ross changed his mind, shifting Cherokee support to the Union cause.

CIVIL WAR WORDS

Five Civilized Tribes: The Chickasaw, Choctaw, Cherokee, Creek, and Seminole Indians were called the Five Civilized Tribes by white men, because they tried to coexist by adopting white customs (such as publishing Indian newspapers, wearing suits, living in houses, and attending missionary schools).

SOLDIERS FROM ABROAD

Although the Civil War was a battle between Americans, there were many foreigners who joined in the war, aiding both the Union and Confederate causes. Many foreigners already lived in America at the time of the war: 4,000,000 in the North, 233,000

in the South. Nearly half had arrived in the years just before the fighting began and were not yet U.S. citizens.

Some immigrants sided with the Union, others with the Confederacy. In both the North and the South there were German, Irish, and French regiments, Scottish battalions, even Swiss, Dutch, and Mexican companies. Some regiments were formed entirely from immigrants, and others mixed foreign soldiers with American soldiers. It was, in fact, a Russian officer, General John Turchin, who led Yankee soldiers in capturing Huntsville, Alabama, from the South.

All the foreign fighters brought symbols of their homeland to camp life and onto the battlefield. These included distinctive clothing and banners, music, and food. One Irish brigade carried a banner with the Confederate flag on one side and a green harp with shamrocks on the reverse.

Although most foreigners fought bravely and many played key roles in the final Union victory, there was also a much higher degree of desertion among foreign troops than native-born soldiers. It was, after all, America's war, and foreign soldiers could return to their homelands when they tired of the fighting.

WOMEN & THE WAR

During the Civil War, the law prohibited women from joining the military. It wasn't until 1942, in fact—during World War II—that females were finally allowed to serve in the U.S. Army. Women, however, were as much a part of the Civil War effort as men. In both the Union and Confederacy, they served in many different ways—as factory workers, fund-raisers, teachers, and nurses. Some women even worked as spies, or disguised themselves as men so they could serve as soldiers!

THE DRAGON WHO HEALED THE SICK

In the mid-nineteenth century most men believed that war was too violent for women, that they would faint from the mere sight of blood and injury. A Massachusetts woman named Dorothea Dix knew better. As soon as fighting broke out, she traveled to Washington, D.C., and requested permission to create an organization of women nurses to aid the Union's sick and wounded. Soon after, she formed the U.S. Army's first professional nursing corps.

Dix, like many people of her day, believed that nurses who were too young or attractive would distract the soldiers from their military duties. Thus, she handpicked her nursing recruits, insisting that they be "plain-looking and at least 30 years old." These tactics soon earned her the nickname Dragon Dix, because she seemed to prefer nurses whose skin was as old and wrinkled as a dragon.

Dorothea Dix played an important part in helping Northern soldiers survive the war. If she was a "dragon," this was one dragon who knew how to heal.

THE BATTLEFIELD ANGEL

Another Massachusetts woman, a schoolteacher named Clara Barton, also gained fame for aiding the Union's sick and wounded. Unlike Dorothea Dix, however, Barton insisted on helping soldiers on the battlefront, and her bravery under fire earned her the nickname The Angel of the Battlefield.

When the Civil War erupted, Barton decided to visit the local hospitals, bringing soap, bandages, and home-cooked food to the soldiers recovering there. After she saw how badly injured the men were, she realized how much more could be done for them if they were treated while still on the battlefield.

Barton wrote letters to the federal government, asking for permission to travel to the battlefront, where she could help stop wounds from bleeding and feed the hungry soldiers. At first she was refused, but Barton was persistent, and the Union Army eventually granted her use of a supply wagon to carry her supplies.

CIVIL WAR WORDS

Sanitary Commission: The U.S. Sanitary Commission began as a charity relief organization, but soon grew to become an aid for wounded soldiers. It opened hospitals and ran mobile medical wagons known as flying depots.

Clara Barton tended soldiers the moment she arrived on the battlefield. "I went in," she explained, "while the battle raged." Often she would care for soldiers while under gunfire. At the Battle of Antietam (September 1862), a soldier she was feeding was killed by an enemy bullet that had first passed right through her sleeve!

During the war, Clara Barton was called a *Sanitary Commission* of one. In 1881 she founded the National Society of the Red Cross (called the American Red Cross today), an organization providing emergency aid in peacetime as well as during war.

A WOMAN NAMED MOSES

One of the Union's most effective weapons against the South was an escaped slave named Harriet Tubman. During the war, she worked for the Union Army as a cook, a laundress, a nurse, and a spy. Her greatest success, however, was kept a secret from both the Union and Confederate armies. Harriet Tubman, known as Moses (after the Jewish leader who guided his enslaved people to freedom many centuries before), led hundreds of her fellow slaves to freedom in the North.

Tubman was born a slave named Araminta in Maryland in 1820. She was cruelly mistreated as a child and wished she could be free. She had heard stories from other slaves of something called the Underground Railroad. This wasn't a real railroad. It was a long line of safe places where escaped slaves could hide as they sneaked north toward freedom. Tubman didn't know if such a thing really existed, but she decided to find out. In 1849, with the help of the Underground Railroad, she escaped to freedom in Philadelphia, Pennsylvania.

But her own liberty wasn't enough for Harriet Tubman, since her friends and family were still living as slaves. Over the course of the war, she made 19 dangerous journeys back into slave territory to lead others to freedom.

★ ★ ★ ★ ★ ★ **THE LITTLE DRUMMER GIRL** ★ ★ ★ ★ ★ ★

There are many stories of young boys who were mustered into the Union and Confederate armies as drummer boys. There was also at least one young girl who refused to be kept out of the action, although records reveal no more than her first name, Emily.

Originally from Brooklyn, New York, Emily was living in Michigan when the Civil War began. Like other women who wanted to join the army, Emily cut off her hair and disguised herself as a boy. She then enlisted as a drummer boy in the Union's Army of the Cumberland.

Unfortunately, Emily was killed during the Battle of Lookout Mountain, Tennessee (November 1863). It was then that her true identity was discovered. Official records tell no more.

★ ★

PRIVATE FRANK THOMPSON, MASTER OF DISGUISE

In 1861 Private Frank Thompson joined the 2nd Michigan Infantry and, due to his ability to disguise himself, soon became one of Union general George B. McClellan's most trusted spies. During the North's Peninsular Campaign, Private Thompson painted his face black, put on a wig, and sneaked behind enemy lines disguised as a slave. At one point during the war, he even passed himself off as a Confederate infantryman. His greatest disguise, however, remained a secret until 1883, long after the war was over. Unknown even to his Union compatriots, Private Frank Thompson was, in fact, Sara Edmonds, a Canadian immigrant . . . and a woman!

CRAZY BET, THE UNION SPY

One of the Union's most successful spies was not only unarmed, untrained, and a woman, but a Southerner who lived in Richmond, Virginia—the Confederate capital itself. Her name was Elizabeth Van Lew.

Van Lew was the daughter of a successful Virginia family. She loved her home in the South, but after returning from school in Philadelphia, she grew to believe that slavery was wrong. Soon after, she convinced her parents to free the family's slaves.

When Virginia joined the Confederacy, Elizabeth decided

to do what she could to aid the Union cause. She began to carry food and medicine to captured Yankee soldiers held in nearby Libby Prison. Other Richmond citizens thought her head had been filled with crazy ideas while away at college, and so they began to call her Crazy Bet.

Van Lew soon realized that people would leave her alone if they believed she was crazy. She began to talk to herself while walking through the streets. She let her hair fall wild and dressed in tattered clothes.

Over time, she developed a complex system of gathering information from prisoners to give to Union troops. Van Lew left books for the soldiers to read, and they would underline words that she could string together into detailed messages. Van Lew also convinced her mother to help her build a network of informers throughout Richmond. Van Lew then devised a relay system to make certain all the information she and her informers gathered was sent to Union generals.

After the Union Army invaded Richmond (near the end of the war), General Grant made a special trip to visit Elizabeth Van Lew. "You have sent me the most valuable information received from Richmond during the war," he said gratefully.

DID YOU KNOW...

Mittens Once Stopped the Fighting?

At the start of the war, both Union and Confederate armies lacked enough food and clothing to adequately supply their troops. So, in 1861, Quaker women from Pennsylvania decided to help the Union soldiers by knitting them a large supply of mittens. The Northern soldiers gratefully accepted the gift, eager to keep their hands warm during the cold winter months. But none of the mittens had been sewn with separate trigger fingers, and since the soldiers were reluctant to take their mittens off once their hands were warm, they were unable to fire their guns!

THE SPY WHOM EVERYBODY KNEW

Belle Boyd was probably the Civil War's most famous female spy—but not because she was the best at her job. In fact, because so many people knew who she was, Belle Boyd was unable to get much spying done at all!

Boyd began her career like many other women during the war. The daughter of a Virginia farmer, she helped transport medicine to wounded Confederate soldiers, often through Union battle lines. But it wasn't long before the adventuresome Boyd began sneaking messages about the location of Union troops to Rebel commanders as well. She even gave General Stonewall Jackson the information he needed to launch a successful surprise attack on the Northern Army at Front Royal, Virginia.

This spy work, at least, was what Boyd claimed to have done. No one could be sure if the daring missions she described were real or imagined. The only thing people knew for certain was that Boyd loved to talk about her spying. And, with the help of the newspapers—which called her the Siren of the Shenandoah and the Rebel Joan of Arc—she soon became a well-known celebrity.

Even though there was little evidence of her actual spying, the Union arrested Boyd numerous times during the war. Each arrest just led to greater publicity, which, of course, Boyd did not seem to mind. Eventually, Union officials, tired of the whole affair, deported the troublesome Rebel to faraway Canada, which was neutral territory.

Belle Boyd's fame and fortune continued after the war ended. She published her life story and afterward toured the United States reciting dramatic stories of her war days. She called her traveling show *The Perils of a Spy*.

FLAGS & BANNERS

Flags played an important role in the Civil War, and those who carried them were often considered a regiment's finest soldiers. Flags helped rally frightened or scattered troops and guided men through the dense battle smoke. But flag carriers were also an easy target for the enemy, and many brave men died while hoisting their regiment's colors aloft.

A DANGEROUS FLAG DESIGN

At the outset of the war, the Confederacy adopted a flag called the Stars and Bars. It was very similar to the Union's Stars and Stripes, featuring a blue field with seven stars (at the time, only seven states had joined the Confederacy) and three wide red-and-white bars, or stripes.

    Southerners liked their new flag. It was still red, white, and blue, but also different enough from the U.S. flag to proclaim their new nation, the Confederate States of America. Almost immediately, however, Southern soldiers discovered their new flag wasn't different enough. In the smoke and confusion of battle, the Stars and Bars looked enough like the Stars and Stripes that Rebels found themselves shooting at each other.

    The Confederacy was forced to redesign their battle flag. They adopted a crossed blue star pattern that eventually came to symbolize the Southern rebellion.

WE'LL TAKE THE STARS, YOU TAKE THE STRIPES

In the North, many people proposed new flags for the divided Union and Confederacy. Samuel Morse, an artist (and the inventor of Morse code), thought that each side might keep half the traditional Stars and Stripes, replacing the missing portion with an empty white field. This way, Morse explained, both North and South would be reminded of what they were missing and wish for the day when the flag, and the country, might be reunited.

President Lincoln would have none of it. The purpose of going to war was to preserve the Union, he explained, and thus the Union's flag had to remain unchanged.

THE FLAGS THAT CHANGED THE WAR

At the Battle of Fredericksburg in December 1862, the Union introduced a new flag-bearing branch of the military, the U.S. Army Signal Corps. These soldiers used small flags to relay coded messages from hilltop to hilltop. It was an invention that changed the way the war was waged from then on.

In the past, messages sent to and from the battlefront had to be carried by horseback, a time-consuming and dangerous task. The Army Signal Corps' flags were a major improvement, because officers could send messages about changing battle conditions, and troops could receive orders quickly.

But there also were dangers to signaling with flags. Opposing troops might decipher a signalman's code and gather information on enemy battle orders. Because of this, binoculars or telescopes that fell into enemy hands were considered more dangerous than rifles. Signal Corps soldiers usually worked in small groups on distant outposts, where they were in constant danger of being overrun and captured by the enemy.

CIVIL WAR INVENTIONS

America has always been a nation devoted to progress, to finding cheaper and more efficient ways to do things. The Civil War sparked an intense explosion of new inventions—tools that modernized the weapons of war.

GUNNING FOR THE UNION

When seven Southern states declared themselves the Confederate States of America in February 1861 (four others joined later), Samuel Colt—the Connecticut gun maker who invented the revolver in 1835—realized the Union would need to fight to hold the nation together. "Run the armory day and night with double sets of hands," he told his workers.

Colt designed new revolvers for the Union Army and Navy, and introduced a new kind of revolving rifle, which allowed Yankee marksmen to fire six shots in place of a Confederate soldier's single bullet.

His factory produced hundreds of thousands of weapons over the course of the war, making Colt the Union's largest supplier of pistols and rifles. His weapons would go on to even greater fame in the postwar years, as settlers headed west into dangerous frontier territory—with their "trusty Colts" close by their sides.

RIVERBOATS ARMED FOR WAR

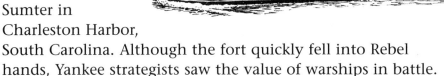

The Civil War began on the water, when Confederate forces attacked Fort Sumter in Charleston Harbor, South Carolina. Although the fort quickly fell into Rebel hands, Yankee strategists saw the value of warships in battle.

Almost immediately, the Union began construction on a new type of weapon, a fleet of iron warships (before the Civil War, ships had been made entirely of wood). Iron warships had to be built strong enough to survive cannon fire from the shoreline, and to carry cannons large enough to destroy Rebel fortifications along the embankment. In spite of all this armament, they had to float lightly enough to sail down rivers that were no more than 10 feet deep!

Some of these ships were used to blockade Southern ports, cutting off Confederate supplies from Europe. Other warships patrolled rivers that ran through the South. Within a period of months, the Union's river fleet—Western Flotilla— controlled the Mississippi, Ohio, and Missouri rivers. The Confederate Army, without access to the iron plating manufactured in the North, was forced to travel on long, exhausting marches over ground.

CONFEDERATE COAL

Few Confederates did more to "rain" death and destruction upon Union forces than the Rains brothers, who revolutionized the use of explosive *munitions* during the war.

General Gabriel Rains had always been interested in explosives. His younger brother, George, made gunpowder for the Confederate Army. Together, they set out to create devices that might give the Confederacy the upper hand over the larger and better-equipped Union Army.

In January 1864 they presented a small device to Confederate president Jefferson Davis. It was a black iron box containing a powerful explosive, designed to look like a simple lump of coal. Confederate agents would only have to sneak aboard Federal warships—disguised either as Union sailors or civilian stowaways—and place one of the explosives in the ship's coal bin. Once shoveled into the boiler, the bomb would cause an explosion large enough to sink the entire warship.

Confederate president Davis called the Rains brothers' device "perfection itself." It was tested immediately, sinking the Confederacy's own ship, the *Greyhound*, which had been captured and was being held by the Union. The brothers went on to build booby traps, mines, and torpedoes for the Confederacy, producing nearly 3,000,000 pounds of gunpowder to fuel their explosive creations.

THE ARTILLERY WAR

Civil War soldiers fought each other at close range, but unlike soldiers in earlier wars, they rarely fought in hand-to-hand combat. Instead, they relied upon their rifles and their brigades' field *artillery*, which consisted of an array of large guns and cannons.

Artillery guns were in use for at least three centuries before the Civil War, but they were inaccurate weapons. At the war's outset, both the North and South were equipped with such unreliable cannons, built in the 1840s and earlier. Munitions experts on both sides set out to improve their armies' field artillery.

CIVIL WAR WORDS

Artillery: Large battlefield guns and cannons, usually anything too large to carry by hand.

Munitions: Military supplies consisting of weapons and ammunition.

Many technological improvements were made. New cannons were manufactured from iron instead of bronze, from which they had been made in the past. This made them much less expensive to produce, since iron was more readily available. New tools allowed gunners to load and fire their cannons twice a minute, much faster than ever before. A spiral groove (called rifling) was added inside a cannon's barrel, to spin a projectile and improve its accuracy. The addition of detailed charts dramatically improved a soldier's ability to aim his artillery weapons.

In the end, artillery cannons became a brigade's most dependable tools of attack and defense. Their new success on the battlefield made the Civil War the bloodiest conflict in America's history.

THE UNION'S DICTATOR

The Union's 110,000 manufacturing factories and 22,000 miles of railroad track gave it a large advantage over the Confederacy, as far as building and transporting large weaponry was concerned. One of the most impressive uses of this advantage was the invention of a 17,120-pound mortar gun capable of firing 200-pound shells a distance of nearly 3 miles—a weapon so heavy that it could only be transported along railroad tracks!

The weapon was dubbed the Dictator, because there was no defense possible in the face of such explosive power. The Union used the Dictator to overtake the town of Petersburg, Virginia, in 1864. An eyewitness described the bursting of a shell as "terrific, an 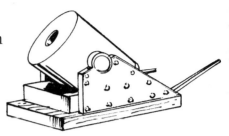 immense crater being formed in the ground where it fell, and earth, stones, and sod (grass) being scattered in every direction, much to the horror of the inhabitants of the place."

THE COFFEE-MILL GUN

One of the deadliest inventions of the Civil War was a rapid-firing weapon called a machine gun, first demonstrated to President Lincoln in June 1861. As the president turned a crank, a continuous stream of bullets dropped from a large bin into the firing chamber. (The bullets did not have to be loaded in by hand one at a time.) "A coffee-mill gun," Lincoln exclaimed, naming the new gun after the way coffee beans drop into a coffee-mill chamber to be ground into coffee.

Lincoln ordered 60 machine guns for the Union Army, but they were rarely used by his battlefield commanders. General Ripley, the man in charge of weaponry for the Union Army, had served for over 50 years and didn't believe machine guns were useful for winning the war. He

CIVIL WAR WORDS

Arsenal: A place where weapons and military supplies are stored; a collection of weapons.

felt the only way to victory was with traditional weapons, and so he placed many of the new guns in storage.

Those soldiers who did use the new weapon reported dramatic success on the battlefield. But it wasn't until August of 1866, more than a year after the Civil War had ended, that the United States Army adopted the machine gun as part of its official *arsenal*.

CODED COMMANDS

One of the greatest dangers in trying to relay orders to troops located in enemy territory was keeping battle commands secret from the enemy. It was bad enough that newspapers reported where soldiers were stationed and published maps of battle sites, but ordinary messages could be intercepted by spies, signal flags could be seen by anyone with a telescope or binoculars, and telegraph lines could be tapped. It seemed the only safe way to send messages to the battlefront was to write them in code.

To code a message meant creating special alphabet wheels, called ciphers, that allowed the scrambled letters to be uncoded (or deciphered). Troops were given cipher wheels that could be adapted for a constantly changing series of codes. These wheels were so valuable that soldiers were expected to destroy them—and themselves, if necessary—before they could be captured by the enemy.

Once the war began, there was little time to invent a complex coding system and train an army already on the move to use it. The Union created their own system, but the Confederacy decided to use an old European system instead. Unfortunately, it was so complex that by the time many messages were deciphered, they were no longer of much use. Some Confederate officers preferred to ignore their ciphers and send runners back to the message-senders to find out what was actually being said!

THE SPY IN THE SKY

The Civil War was considered a "modern" war for many reasons, not least of which was the introduction of aerial reconnaissance (the scouting of enemy terrain and troop locations) in battle. The man most responsible for this innovation was scientist Thaddeus Lowe.

On April 20, 1861, unaware that Southern Rebels had fired on Fort Sumter six days earlier, Lowe launched his hot-air balloon *Enterprise* on a scientific test flight. Strong winds carried him off course, and Lowe landed his balloon in South Carolina. He was promptly arrested as a Union spy. Lowe explained that he was not a soldier and didn't even know the United States was at war. Fortunately, fellow scientists vouched for his peaceful intentions, and he was released.

Lowe offered his services to the Union Army and soon commanded a group of civilian balloonists known as the Union Army's Aeronautics Corps. On 3,000 flights over the next two years, Lowe and his men traveled miles into the sky, relaying information to the ground on enemy positions and troop movements. His balloons became one of the most visible and hated weapons in the Yankee arsenal. Lowe himself quickly became known as "the most shot-at man of the Civil War."

THE BIRTH OF THE CAN OPENER

If the Union Army hadn't needed a way to feed their hungry troops, the can opener may never have become the common household tool it is today.

The tin can was actually invented in England, in 1810, and used for British soldiers' battle rations (food supplies) in the

84

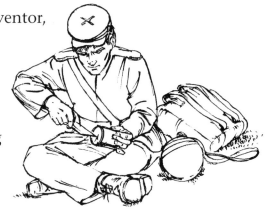

War of 1812. However, the inventor, Peter Durand, never bothered creating a way to open his vacuum-sealed cans. Soldiers were left to improvise, puncturing the cans with bayonets or knives or opening them with gunfire.

Tin cans were brought to America in 1817, and those who used them were also forced to invent their own way to open them. In 1858 Ezra J. Warner of Waterbury, Connecticut, patented the first can-opening device. When the Civil War broke out, the Union Army realized the value of supplying troops with individual meal containers, along with a reliable way of opening the cans. Warner's can opener was purchased and included in each soldier's standard equipment.

THE HOME FRONT

As soldiers marched off to battle, those who stayed at home did what they could to help the war effort. They staffed hospitals, stitched uniforms, worked in factories, and tended the farms. But as the war dragged on, they welcomed any event that might take their minds off the seemingly endless stream of battles. They longed for the day the war would finally be over and their loved ones might return home.

A CAPITAL TRANSFORMED

Before the Civil War, the nation's capital, Washington, D.C., was still a small city. It had been under construction since 1800, but few buildings surrounded the White House. Much of the land was swamp or pasture. The Washington Monument was unfinished, and so was the Capitol dome of Congress.

When the war broke out, the capital city was suddenly transformed into a busy, crowded place. Most of the Union's military supplies were stored at the Washington Arsenal. Thousands of troops jammed the streets, drilling and marching in formation. Hospitals sprung up everywhere. Herds of cattle were corralled by the Potomac River in order to provide a steady supply of beef and milk for the troops. Within a period of months, Washington, D.C., became the focus point for the whole Northern war campaign.

In spite of this frenzied activity, President Lincoln insisted that the construction of the capital continue during the war. Building for the future, said Lincoln, sent a message to all Americans: "We intend the Union shall go on."

A HERO'S WELCOME

At the outset of the Civil War, most people expected the fighting to end quickly. Soldiers enlisted for tours of duty lasting only 90 days. The first regiments of soldiers returning home were welcomed as heroes and given large patriotic celebrations.

After their first tour of duty, most soldiers quickly reenlisted and returned to the battlefield to continue the fight. As the years dragged on, however, and many more soldiers were wounded or killed in combat, hometown celebrations were mixed with feelings of sadness and loss. The number of new recruits dwindled and mandatory military drafts were instituted in both the North and South. By 1863 soldiers were required to fight for years at a time, instead of months.

At the end of the war, any soldier who had managed to survive the war was considered a hero, and simply returning home was celebration enough.

RIOTS IN THE STREETS

Not all citizens in the North and South supported the war effort. At times, people at home became so fed up with the effects of the war that they rioted in the streets.

When the Civil War began, President Lincoln issued a call for volunteer soldiers to put down the Southern rebellion. Two years later, heavy Union losses in the battlefield forced the U.S. government to pass the Federal Draft Act. All men between the ages of 18 and 45 were considered eligible for military service. It was the first formal draft in the history of the country.

For $300, however, a person could hire a substitute to take his place. Because this favored the wealthy and forced poor people to fight, many people thought the draft was unfair.

On July 13, 1863, in New York City, public anger turned to protest. As the first draftees' names were called, a mob of 70,000 people rioted in the streets. They destroyed the draft office, burned buildings, stole from stores, and attacked the homes of rich people. For three days they raged against the police and Federal soldiers.

In the South, citizens also staged wild public protests, but for a different reason. Life was hard in the Confederacy. The Union blockade of Southern ports had made even the most ordinary items, such as paper and soap, unavailable. What supplies there were had to be sent to the troops in the battlefield. Back home, there often was little or no food to eat.

On March 15, 1863, a group of citizens in Salisbury, North Carolina, decided to take the matter into their own hands. Carrying axes and knives, they marched through the streets, searching for any scrap of food to eat. More people joined in, and the protest spread to Richmond, Virginia, where the large mob attacked banks and stores.

President Jefferson Davis raced to the scene. He pleaded

with his people to return to their homes. He urged them to fight for the Confederacy instead of against it. The people listened, and the riot was over.

WHEN JEFFERSON DAVIS WAS WORTH 5¢

Confederate president Jefferson Davis is the only person ever pictured on an American postage stamp while still alive.

Soon after the war began, Confederate postmaster general John Reagan decided that Confederate postage stamps should commemorate important Southern figures like Jefferson Davis. Reagan hired a sculptor named Frederick Volck, who sketched pictures of Davis while the president was in church. But when the stamp was finally issued, many people thought the picture looked a little bit too much like Abraham Lincoln, and so President Davis's stamp was withdrawn from use.

After the war, many Southerners remembered their president's five-cent memorial. A Confederate veteran, passing Jefferson Davis on a Richmond, Virginia, street one day, said, "Are you Mister Davis?"

"I am," answered the ex-president.

"Well, by God," thundered the man, "I thought you looked like a postage stamp."

THE SACK OF FLOUR THAT DESERVED A MEDAL

One of the greatest contributors to the Union war effort was not a soldier, an inventor, or a congressman . . . but, in fact, a simple sack of flour!

On October 31, 1864, President Lincoln admitted Nevada to statehood, knowing its rich stores of silver would help fund the Union's war effort. Nevada citizens were enjoying a mining boom and many of them had become very wealthy. During a local election in Austin, Nevada, the two candidates for mayor made a friendly bet. Each agreed that the loser of the election would carry a 50-pound sack of flour to the winner, as a gift. Reuel Gridley, the Democratic candidate, lost. As promised, he promptly delivered the sack of flour to his opponent, Dr. H. S. Herrick.

But Herrick didn't really *need* the flour, so Gridley suggested they auction it off to the highest bidder and donate the money to the U.S. Sanitary Commission.

Gridley himself started the bidding by offering $300 for the sack of flour. It was then auctioned again, with local miners joining in the bidding. By the end of the day, the sack of flour had raised $5,000. Gridley continued to auction the bag of flour, traveling through Nevada to California, then all the way back across the United States to New York City. Citizens all across the nation gave generously to aid the Northern war effort.

When Gridley finally presented the bag of flour to the Sanitary Commission in St. Louis, Missouri, it had earned over $270,000. The flour was then used to bake small cakes, which were sold for $1 each.

THE GETTYSBURG ADDRESS

The Battle of Gettysburg (July 1–3, 1863) was the bloodiest conflict of the Civil War, lasting three days and adding over 50,000 Union and Confederate soldiers to the growing list of casualties. It was also a turning point in the war. Even though

89

both North and South lost similar numbers of men, the Battle of Gettysburg stopped the Rebel invasion of the North and began the Union Army's long march toward victory.

On November 19, 1863, the fields where the battle was fought were converted into a memorial, a national cemetery honoring the Union soldiers who had fallen there. President Lincoln was asked to say a few words of introduction at the dedication ceremony. The speech he delivered has been remembered ever since as the Gettysburg Address:

CIVIL WAR WORDS

Fourscore: A *score* is an old word meaning "twenty"; *fourscore and seven years* means "eighty-seven years."

"Fourscore *and seven years ago our fathers brought forth on this continent, a new nation, conceived in Liberty, and dedicated to the proposition that all men are created equal.*

"*Now we are engaged in a great civil war, testing whether that nation or any nation so conceived and so dedicated can long endure. We are met on a great battlefield of that war. We have come to dedicate a portion of that field, as a final resting place for those who here gave their lives that that nation might live. It is altogether fitting and proper that we should do this.*

"*But, in a larger sense, we cannot dedicate—we cannot consecrate —we cannot hallow—this ground. The brave men, living and dead, who struggled here, have consecrated it far above our poor power to add or detract. The world will little note nor long remember what we say here, but it can never forget what they did here. It is for us, the living, rather to be dedicated here to the unfinished work which they who fought here have thus far so nobly advanced. It is rather for us to be here dedicated to the great task remaining before us—that from these honored dead we take increased devotion to that cause for which they gave the last full measure of devotion; that we here highly resolve that these dead shall not have died in vain; that this nation, under God, shall have a new birth of freedom; and that government of the people, by the people, for the people, shall not perish from the earth.*"

THE WAR THAT GAVE US INCOME TAX

Before the Civil War, American citizens paid no income tax. The U.S. government supported itself by placing *tariffs* on imported and exported goods.

But the cost of equipping soldiers with food, clothing, and supplies was very high, and so in 1861, to help fund the war effort, the era of income taxes was born.

CIVIL WAR WORDS

Tariff: A fee or tax imposed by the government on imported or exported goods.

The North's first income tax was a 3 percent toll on annual incomes over $800. Unfortunately, this didn't bring the government enough new money to pay for the growing war effort. Therefore, in 1862, the income tax was expanded to cover all Union citizens. Eight of the Confederacy's eleven states also passed income tax laws. These taxes varied from 1 percent to 15 percent of a person's yearly income.

Income taxes were very unpopular with citizens in both the North and the South. When the war ended, the income tax law was repealed by Congress. Eventually, however, income taxes would return. On February 3, 1913, Congress passed the 16th Amendment to the Constitution, which made income taxes a permanent part of the federal financial system.

THREE ORPHANS FROM GETTYSBURG

After the Battle of Gettysburg, the bloodiest battle of the Civil War, the more than 50,000 dead had to be buried quickly, to prevent the spread of disease. Sometimes it was hard to identify each of the fallen soldiers before they were buried. Family members often didn't know what had happened to missing loved ones who were lost in the fighting.

One Union soldier lying dead on Gettysburg's battlefield was found with a small photograph of three young children held in his hand. Since he had no other identification, Federal officials made thousands of copies of the picture and posted them throughout the Union, asking whether anyone recognized the children. Everyone talked about the unknown soldier's three lost orphans, but no one knew who they were. Somebody even offered to give $50 to the person who wrote the best poem about the orphans. The winner's lyrics were turned into a popular song.

People everywhere bought copies of the orphans' song and photo. Finally, a woman said she recognized the children. The fallen soldier was identified as Sergeant Amos Humiston of the 154th New York Infantry.

After the war, the profits from the sales of the photo and song were used to found the Soldiers' Orphans' Home in Gettysburg, Pennsylvania, in Sergeant Humiston's honor. His three children were among the first orphans to go to school there.

★ ★ ★ ★ ★ ★ **A SONG TO END THE WAR** ★ ★ ★ ★ ★ ★

One of the most famous American folk songs to emerge from the Civil War is "When Johnny Comes Marching Home," written in 1863 by Patrick Sarsfield Gilmore. The song comforted Southerners by making them think of the days ahead, when the war would at last be over and their soldiers, Johnny Rebs, would finally come marching home.

> *"When Johnny comes marching home again,*
> *Hurrah! Hurrah!*
> *We'll give him a hearty welcome then,*
> *Hurrah! Hurrah!*
> *The men will cheer, the boys will shout;*
> *The ladies they will all turn out,*
> *And we'll all feel gay,*
> *When Johnny comes marching home."*

★ ★

AFTER THE WAR

Confederate general Lee's surrender to Union general Grant at Appomattox Court House, Virginia, on April 9, 1865 brought an end to the war at last. And with the end of the war came a new beginning for the nation. Americans were asked to put aside their hatreds and work together to build a common future. The legacies of the Civil War carry on to this day.

AFTERMATH

After four long years of fighting, Americans had many different reactions to the end of the war. Some Northerners wanted revenge against the South, while others had sympathy for their fallen foes. Scattered Rebels refused to surrender and hid in the hills, promising to continue the fight. Many ex-slaves headed west, to start a new life on land they could call their own. Most people were just glad that the war was over and eager to get on with their lives.

LINCOLN WAS A FAN OF JOHN WILKES BOOTH

John Wilkes Booth is best remembered as the Southerner who brutally assassinated President Lincoln on April 14, 1865, five days after the end of the Civil War. Throughout his life, however, Booth was a famous and popular actor. In fact, President Abraham Lincoln was among his many fans!

The Booth family was the most famous acting family in America at this time. John Wilkes Booth's father, Junius Brutus Booth, was a great Shakespearean actor. All four of his boys acted as well, as did their wives. John, in particular, was loved in both the North and the South for his fiery and dramatic performances.

President Lincoln, himself, enjoyed the theater and attended stage productions often. In November 1863 he was entranced by John Wilkes Booth's performance in a play called *Marble Heart*. But his love of theater was to be his downfall. While Lincoln attended a production of *Our American Cousin* at Ford's Theater, Booth, determined to avenge the Confederacy's defeat, shot the president as he sat in his theater box. Lincoln died early the next day.

DID YOU KNOW...

Booth Once Saved Lincoln's Life?

Everybody knows that John Wilkes Booth assassinated Abraham Lincoln, but did you know that Booth once saved Lincoln's life? It's true. But it was Edwin Thomas Booth, John's brother, who saved Robert Todd Lincoln, the president's oldest son.

During the war years, Robert Todd Lincoln was a student at Harvard University. One evening the young Lincoln was thrown off balance by a pressing crowd of passengers as he was waiting to board a train to Washington, D.C. He fell onto the train tracks below.

Another passenger standing on the platform quickly pulled Robert up by his jacket before he could be crushed by an oncoming train. "Upon turning to thank my rescuer," said Robert, "I saw it was Edwin Booth." A famous and well-liked actor, Booth was known to many Northerners.

Years later, when Edwin's brother John killed the president, Edwin shared the world's shock, horror, and shame in the crime.

"ALL INDEED IS LOST"

When Confederate general Lee surrendered his army at Appomattox Court House on April 9, 1865, the Civil War was officially over—but the stubborn Rebel president, Jefferson Davis, was not ready to give up. On May 2 Davis gathered his remaining military leaders to discuss how to continue the fight.

Davis's military commanders were shocked at the idea. The war had ended, the Southern people were devastated, their cities were destroyed, and the Union Army was victorious. Hearing all this, the saddened Confederate president whispered, "All indeed is lost."

Meanwhile, those in the North were eager to heal the nation's wounds. It had been two weeks since President Lincoln was assassinated by the Southerner John Wilkes Booth. Many people believed Booth had killed the president on Jefferson Davis's orders. The new president, Andrew Johnson, therefore issued a $100,000 reward for Jefferson Davis's capture.

After his meeting with his commanders, Davis made his way to Irwinsville, Georgia, to meet his wife, Varina, unaware of the reward posted for his capture. On May 10 he awoke to discover Union soldiers had surrounded his tent. Davis decided to face his captors. Varina, knowing it was cold outside, threw her shawl over her husband as he left the tent.

That small act was to do more damage to Jefferson Davis's spirit than almost anything else that happened during the Civil War. Rumors circulated that Davis had been caught trying to flee while hiding in his wife's clothes. People laughed and mocked him all over the world. Davis was shocked that anyone believed *he* could do something so "unbecoming a soldier and a gentleman." He knew his reputation as the proud protector of the Southern cause was ruined forever.

A NEW PRESIDENT

When President Lincoln was assassinated on April 14, 1865, vice president Andrew Johnson was sworn in as the nation's 17th president. Even though the Civil War had ended five days earlier, President Johnson was faced with a difficult task: rebuilding the South and reuniting all Americans into a single nation.

President Johnson was a good man for the job. He had been born in the South, in Raleigh, North Carolina, so he understood what life was like for people in the Southern states. He also knew what it was like to be poor. His father had died when he was only three, and Andrew Johnson worked to help support his family instead of going to school. At age 12 he moved to Tennessee and became a tailor's apprentice.

When he was 16, Johnson opened a tailor shop of his own, and within a few years he was popular enough to be elected mayor of Greeneville, Tennessee. He continued to serve in politics, winning election to Congress in 1843, Tennessee governor in 1853, and the U.S. Senate in 1857. When Tennessee joined the Confederacy in 1862, Andrew Johnson was the only Southern senator to pledge allegiance to the Union. He became President Lincoln's vice president during the 1864 election.

THE ANDERSONVILLE SAVAGE

While many Northerners were willing to pardon their Confederate brothers for participating in the rebellion, there were some Southerners who could not go unpunished. One of those was the commander of the Confederacy's most brutal prison camp, Andersonville. He was Captain Henry Wirz, commonly known as the Andersonville savage.

Surviving Union soldiers told stories of the daily horrors—beatings, murders, and starvation—endured by prisoners at Andersonville. Northerners were outraged. Wirz was soon captured and charged with "murder in violation of the laws and customs of war." He proclaimed his innocence, but after 148 eyewitnesses presented evidence against him, Wirz was sentenced to hang.

On November 10, 1865, the day of execution had arrived. Wirz climbed up the scaffold steps. His crimes and sentence were read to the crowd. Asked if he had any last words, Wirz shot back: "I know what orders are, Major. I am being hanged for obeying them."

Wirz's body was buried on the Washington Arsenal grounds.

THE GRANDEST PARADE

One of the last great acts of the Union's victorious army was also one of the most enjoyable. Before the soldiers disbanded and went their separate ways, President Johnson summoned them to Washington, D.C., for a military victory parade. He called this parade The Grand Review.

With the president, his cabinet, and his military generals proudly watching, 150,000 troops marched in formation down the street. There were so many soldiers that it took two complete days to see them all. Throughout the march, grateful crowds cheered and waved their brave soldiers onward.

"The very air seemed freighted with gladness," said one of the soldiers. "I felt that the pleasures of that day fully repaid me for all the hardships, privations, dangers, and suffering that I had endured during all those years of strife and carnage." To many soldiers, being welcomed home let them know that the war was over at last, and the nation was grateful for their service.

97

★ ★ ★ ★ ★ ★ ★ ★ **NEW AMENDMENTS** ★ ★ ★ ★ ★ ★ ★ ★ ★

There have been many *Constitutional amendments* since the Constitution was written in 1789. The first 10 amendments are commonly called the Bill of Rights, because they formed the basis for what Americans consider their basic rights: freedom of speech, freedom of religion, the right to bear arms, and so on.

The period immediately after the Civil War was an era that granted new rights and freedoms to many Americans. In order for these freedoms to be upheld, they had to be included as amendments to the U.S. Constitution:

13th Amendment (1865): Outlawed slavery throughout the United States and any of its territories or possessions.

14th Amendment (1868): Granted equal protection under the law to all U.S. citizens. Also allowed male citizens of each state to vote, and run for public office, as long as they had not been convicted of any crime or rebellion against the United States. *(Note: Women were not yet granted the right to vote.)*

15th Amendment (1870): Declared that any male citizen was allowed to vote, regardless of race or former slave status.

A CONGRESSMAN FROM ABOVE

In the difficult years after the Civil War, President Johnson worked hard to reunite the country and rebuild the South. But many people thought he was not doing enough to help newly freed blacks. One of Johnson's loudest critics was Thaddeus Stevens, a congressman from Pennsylvania.

Stevens argued for new laws that would change the way the South was governed. He wanted to give more power to the large black population. "The foundations must be broken up and relaid," he said, "or all our blood and treasure have been spent in vain." Even though President Johnson passed the 13th and

14th Amendments to the Constitution—which outlawed slavery and gave black citizens the opportunity to open businesses or run for public office—Thaddeus Stevens wanted to punish slaveholders and give poor blacks even greater opportunities to succeed.

On August 11, 1868, just as the campaign was getting under way for the November elections, Congressman Stevens died. Pennsylvania's Republican Party knew Stevens would have fought

CIVIL WAR WORDS

Constitutional amendment: An addition to, or change in, the basic laws of our country, as written in the U.S. Constitution. New amendments can be added with the approval of two-thirds of the Senate and the House of Representatives, or three-fourths of America's states.

for reelection, to continue his crusade for black Americans. The party decided to honor Stevens by including his name on the ballot—even though he had been dead for three months!

Political opponents laughed at the Republicans, calling Stevens a Corpse for Congress. Pennsylvania voters, however, felt a loyalty to Stevens—and his cause—that even death could not destroy. He was reelected by a wide margin, although a substitute had to serve in his place and fight for his cause.

RECONSTRUCTION BEGINS

The decade after the Civil War was known as Reconstruction. Not only did the nation have to be reunited, but much of the South had been destroyed and needed to be rebuilt.

In 1867 Congress passed the Reconstruction Acts, which

Devastated remains of Richmond, Virginia, one of the South's largest cities.

listed rules that Confederate states were required to obey before being granted full and equal status in the Union again.

Each state had to write a new state constitution, granting all black men the right to vote and be elected to office. They also had to ratify (approve) the 14th Amendment, which said that Southern war veterans and Confederate government officeholders would not be able to vote or hold office, since they had been guilty of open rebellion against the United States.

During Reconstruction, many Northern businessmen, educators, and politicians moved to the Southern states to help form new governments or assist ex-slaves in making new lives. These Northerners were often called *carpetbaggers,* and they joined with another group called *scalawags* to help rebuild the nation.

CIVIL WAR WORDS

Carpetbagger: A term applied to Northerners who moved to Southern states to help with Reconstruction. The name carpetbagger referred to inexpensive suitcases made from pieces of carpet that many of the Northerners carried.

Scalawag: A term applied to native Southerners who worked with Northerners and blacks to rebuild the Southern states.

HATRED WEARS A HOOD

There were some white Southerners who did not want to accept the regulations of Reconstruction. Even though the war was over, they still believed in the Confederacy and refused to think of blacks as free and equal Americans. Since the 14th Amendment prohibited them from holding elected office, these people formed a secret organization to fight for their beliefs. They called this organization the Ku Klux Klan, or KKK.

The Ku Klux Klan was led by Nathan Bedford Forrest, a Confederate general during the Civil War. However, most Klan members were unknown, since they wore white robes and hoods to hide their identities. The Klan staged nighttime raids on black homes and businesses, burning property and threatening black people with further violence. Sometimes they did more than threaten ex-slaves; many black people were killed by Klansmen.

The KKK was disbanded in 1869–71, and a second Klan was revived in 1915. Members of the Klu Klux Klan have continued their illegal and hateful practices to this day, but the list of people the KKK persecutes now includes Catholics, Jews, and many other people.

"FREEDOM WASN'T NO DIFFERENCE"

When the Civil War ended, most slaves hoped freedom would bring instant prosperity. "We thought we was going to be richer than the white folks," said one ex-slave, "'cause we was stronger and knowed how to work." In reality, however, after more than two centuries of bondage, black Americans found that work was hard to find, and few Southerners wanted to grant them the equality they were promised by law.

With nowhere else to turn, many ex-slaves continued to work for their former masters, earning a few dollars per week or a small percentage of the crop. "Freedom wasn't no difference I knows of," said one black worker. Though many ex-slaves married and began new families, they found their postwar lives to be very much like their days in slavery.

In 1870, when Congress passed the 15th Amendment, and all black citizens were guaranteed the right to vote, another promise of freedom and prosperity was made. But in 1898 the state of Louisiana enacted what was called a grandfather clause. This was an extra law that granted the right to vote only to those black citizens whose grandfathers had *also* been able to vote. The grandfather clause meant that all former slaves would not be allowed to vote, and neither would their children or grandchildren.

By the turn of the century, the grandfather clause had also been adopted by Georgia, Alabama, Virginia, Oklahoma, and North Carolina. It wasn't until 1915 that the U.S. Supreme Court declared the grandfather clause illegal and returned the right to vote to all black Americans.

RECONSTRUCTION ENDS

During the 1877 presidential election, people who supported Reconstruction claimed that those who opposed it cheated at the polls (by destroying ballots and casting more votes than were allowed). The apparent winner, Democratic candidate Samuel J. Tilden, had promised to end Reconstruction and grant more power to former leaders of the Confederacy. But many people believed Tilden had not won the election fairly and his opponent, Republican Rutherford B. Hayes, should become president instead. Congress appointed a commission to investigate the election. The commission proposed a compromise—called the Compromise of 1877—which appointed Rutherford B. Hayes to the presidency instead of Tilden, as long as Hayes promised to bring the Reconstruction era to an end.

In addition, the Compromise of 1877 allowed former slave owners to reclaim property that had been seized by Federal troops during the war. Confederate veterans were once again allowed to vote and stand for public office. It was the end of government protection and assistance for many black Americans.

A NEW AMERICA

In the second half of the nineteenth century, America grew and changed faster than ever before. The machines of industry that fueled the war sparked a second industrial revolution. Many black people were going to school and working as free Americans for the first time. And both blacks and whites were joining the already large numbers of settlers moving westward into the nation's vast uncharted territories. The spirit of progress was everywhere. It was the beginning of a new America—a nation with its sights set on the future.

INVENTING THE MODERN WORLD

The postwar years were an age of mechanical tinkering. Businesses were growing, and new homes and towns were being built in faraway locations. Americans were eager for machines that could keep them in touch with each other and make their daily lives easier.

American industry was ready to meet their needs. Many new factories had been built to aid the Union war effort, and large numbers of men and women had been trained to work in them. The new techniques of mass production and interchangeable parts produced products more efficiently and more inexpensively. In the decades after 1865, all these resources were turned toward peaceful ends—to create industry and inventions that would forever change the nation.

New shoe-making, cloth-cutting, and sewing machines cut down labor time dramatically. A wireless telegraph and the first typewriter were invented. Streets were paved with asphalt, and the first steam-run automobile appeared. An underground subway was introduced. Most importantly, the transcontinental railroad was completed to transport new goods quickly across the rapidly growing nation.

A NEW STRUGGLE FOR EQUALITY

Blacks weren't the only Americans to strive for greater equality in the postwar years. Soldiers returned home to find a new struggle had begun, often in their own homes. America's women grew stronger because of their contributions to the war effort. As soldiers, spies, nurses, and factory workers, they had proved they were the equals of men.

The Declaration of Independence stated "all men are created equal." In the postwar years, women everywhere—often uneducated, unable to vote, and banned from many jobs—were ready to fight for equal rights of their own. The era of female suffrage, the struggle for equal pay and equal voting rights, had begun.

Examples of women's achievements were everywhere. In 1865 Mary Harris Thompson founded the Chicago Hospital for Women and Children, becoming the leading female surgeon of her day. In 1866 Dr. Lucy Beaman Hobbs Taylor became America's first female dentist, and Susan B. Anthony helped found the American Equal Rights Association. Mary Louise Booth became the editor of a new magazine designed for women, *Harper's Bazaar,* in 1867.

However, most women found themselves as oppressed as before the war. In the late 1860s Lincoln's Republican Party passed the 14th and 15th Amendments, which granted freedom and the right to vote to blacks and other minorities, but not to women. Not until the 19th Amendment was passed, in 1920, would women finally gain that right.

A CHANCE TO LEARN THE ABCs AT LAST

When 4,000,000 slaves were granted their freedom at the end of the Civil War, less than 150,000 of them knew how to read or write. Such basic knowledge had been forbidden by white owners, who believed an educated slave was dangerous.

In the decade after the war, the Freedmen's Bureau—a Federal agency formed to aid and protect newly free blacks—opened 965 new schools to give black citizens an education, and most ex-slaves leaped at the chance. Some slaves sold their old handcuffs and leg irons as scrap metal to help pay for books and supplies. Booker T. Washington, an ex-slave who would one day establish a black vocational school called the Tuskegee Institute, wrote: "It was a whole race trying to go to school. Few were too young, and none were too old to make an attempt to learn."

With so few educated blacks, most teachers in these new black schools were white, usually missionaries from the North. But the Freedmen's Bureau's goal was clear: Within a few years, it hoped that a whole new generation of black educators would rise up to help their people achieve their potential as free and educated Americans.

AMERICA'S FIRST BLACK SENATOR

Before the Civil War, few congressmen did more to promote black inequality than the senator from Mississippi, Jefferson Davis. When Davis resigned to lead the Confederacy, he left his congressional seat empty. After the war, the first senator to reclaim Davis's Senate seat was Hiram Revels—America's first black senator.

Born a free man, Hiram Revels devoted his life to fighting for freedom and equality for others. An ordained minister of the African Methodist Church, he served as a Union chaplain during the war. When Mississippi joined the Confederacy, Revels crossed into Missouri, a border state, and helped recruit regiments of black soldiers for the Union Army. In 1863 he founded a school for free black men in St. Louis, Missouri.

After the war, Revels was elected to the Mississippi State Senate, where he argued passionately for equality and the full return of civil rights to ex-Confederate citizens—including his fellow blacks. In 1870 Revels won election to the U.S. Senate and filled the seat once vacated by his foe, Jefferson Davis.

CIVIL WAR LEGACIES

As the years passed, the Civil War held a special place in all Americans' hearts. Veterans of both the Union and the Confederacy were hailed as American patriots. They were called brothers who had had a long battle, each fighting for a vision of a country they loved. Even today the legacy of the Civil War lives on.

THE 400-FOOT BATTLE MEMORIAL

The two-day Battle of Shiloh (April 6–7, 1862) was one of the bloodiest confrontations of the entire Civil War. It is fitting, then, that many of the soldiers lost in battle were given a memorial like no other—a detailed painting of their great struggle, on a canvas stretching 50 feet high and 400 feet long!

The Battle of Shiloh began when Confederate forces under the command of Generals P.G.T. Beauregard and Albert Sidney Johnston staged a surprise attack on General Grant's Union Army along the Tennessee River. On the first day of fighting, a detachment of 5,000 Federal soldiers bravely defended an area known as the Hornet's Nest. Over the course of six hours the Union soldiers held their ground, gradually dying one by one, until they were overwhelmed by the larger Confederate Army. Their heroic struggle, however, had given General Grant enough time to gather reinforcements and mount a counterattack, which eventually led to Union victory.

Twenty years after the war, a French painter named Théophile Poilpot decided to create a memorial to the Hornet's Nest's brave defenders. He began by photographing the battlefield and gathering weapons, banners, and uniforms used in the fighting. Poilpot met with hundreds of Shiloh's survivors and collected photos of soldiers killed in battle.

Using all this memorabilia, Poilpot created a realistic painting of the Battle of Shiloh, showing scenes as described by its participants. Faces of individual soldiers were painted in detail. When it was completed, Poilpot then constructed a special circular display gallery for his work, and created a 360-degree diorama by placing realistic props in front of the painted scene.

To those who saw Poilpot's creation, the Battle of Shiloh had been recreated. The work was an instant success and people everywhere clamored for a glimpse of the heroic battle. Then, while on tour, the canvas vanished without a trace. Fortunately, Henry H. Bennett, a photographer, had taken pictures of the show, and those photos survive to this day.

CIVIL WAR VETERAN & PRESIDENT, TOO

In addition to Abraham Lincoln, there were seven Civil War veterans who were elected president of the United States:

- **Andrew Johnson, 17th president (1865–1869).** Even though he was from Tennessee, a Confederate state, Johnson served the Union as a brigadier general. He replaced Hannibal Hamlin as vice president under Lincoln and became president after Lincoln's assassination on April 15, 1865.

- **Ulysses S. Grant, 18th president (1869–1877).** Grant began the war as a lieutenant colonel, but he was promoted to lieutenant general and then to commanding general of the Union Army. He became America's highest-ranking general on July 25, 1866.

- **Rutherford B. Hayes, 19th president (1877–1881).** A major in the 23rd Ohio Regiment, Hayes quickly rose to brevet major general. In 1864 he was elected to Congress, but he refused to accept the position while the country was at war. After the Confederacy surrendered, Hayes took his seat in Congress at last.

- **James A. Garfield, 20th president (1881).** Serving as a lieutenant colonel for the 42nd Ohio Regiment, Garfield's success on the battlefield promoted him to major general on September 19, 1863. He was elected to Congress that year and resigned from the Union Army to take his seat in Washington, D.C. He served in Congress until elected president of the United States in 1880.

- **Chester A. Arthur, 21st president (1881–1885).** Arthur served the Union as a war planner in charge of supplying the troops. Arthur began the war as assistant quartermaster general supplying the New York Militia with necessary food and weapons. By the end of the war he had risen to inspector general, in charge of supplying the entire Union Army.

■ **Benjamin Harrison, 23rd president (1889–1893).** As the great-grandson of Benjamin Harrison, signer of the Declaration of Independence, and the grandson of President William Henry Harrison, who had fought in the Indian wars of the 1790s, Benjamin Harrison had a patriotic family heritage to uphold. He began the war as a second lieutenant in the 70th Indiana Regiment and rose to brevet brigadier general by the end of the fighting. In 1880 Harrison was elected to the Senate, where he served a single six-year term.

■ **William McKinley, 25th president (1897–1901).** When the fighting broke out, McKinley enlisted as a private in Company E, 23rd Ohio Regiment (which was commanded by Rutherford B. Hayes). His bravery on the battlefield and devotion to the Union cause promoted him to brevet major by war's end. After resigning from the military, McKinley became a lawyer and was elected to the House of Representatives. He also served as Ohio's governor before being elected president in 1896.

There was one president who lived through this era who managed to *avoid* fighting in the Civil War: Grover Cleveland, America's 22nd and 24th president (1885–1889 and 1893–1897). When drafted by the Union Army, Cleveland hired a substitute for $300 to serve in his place, a practice that was allowed in those days (see p. 87).

★ ★ **THE MAN WHO WOULDN'T BE PRESIDENT** ★ ★

One of the most popular Civil War veterans was Major General William Tecumseh Sherman. During the war, Sherman had been asked to join the Confederacy but served the Union instead, becoming General Grant's most trusted ally.

After the war, when asked if he would consider the possibility of running for president, Sherman refused to discuss it. "If nominated, I will not run," he said. "If elected, I will not serve."

★ ★

GENERAL LEE'S LASTING VICTORY

Did you know that Washington College, named after our country's first president, George Washington, was actually renamed Washington and Lee University to honor Confederate general Robert E. Lee?

After surrendering his Confederate army at Appomattox Court House, Virginia, General Lee was unsure of his future. Would he be tried and hanged as a traitor, or granted a pardon? No matter his own fate, he knew that it was time for America to rebuild itself after so many years of war. "Go home, all you boys who fought with me," he told his troops, "and help to build up the shattered fortunes of our old state."

The federal government did charge Lee with treason, but he was never tried. Instead, he was allowed to retire at the house of a friend near Richmond, Virginia. The trustees of war-ravaged Washington College in nearby Lexington saw an opportunity to give the general another chance to lead *and* rebuild his nation. They asked the old commander to serve as college president. Lee eagerly accepted.

Gathering donations from Americans everywhere, Lee set

about restoring the college, constructing new buildings, landscaping the grounds, and filling the libraries with books. He also hired new teachers and added engineering, law, and chemistry departments.

Five years later the general suffered a stroke. On his death-bed, with friends, family, students, and faculty gathered around, Lee's last words were, "Let the tent be struck." To honor his lasting contributions to the citizens and students of Virginia, the trustees of Washington College decided to rename the school Washington and Lee University. General Lee is buried there.

THE GETTYSBURG REUNION

On July 1, 1913, 50 years after more than 150,000 Union and Confederate soldiers fought the bloodiest battle of the war, the survivors of Gettysburg met to commemorate the anniversary of their historic conflict.

Although most of the Civil War veterans were well past 90 years old by that time, 120 members of Confederate major general George Pickett's division and 180 soldiers of the Union's Philadelphia Brigade formed military ranks 100 feet apart on either side of the same stone wall over which they had battled 50 years before. At 3:15 P.M., exactly the same time that the battle had begun, a flag bearer from each side ran forward and raised the battle flag. The grizzled old enemies charged the wall again . . . and shook hands!

"Your last memories of this field will overlay the earlier ones," said a speaker that day. "It will no longer picture itself as a field of carnage and suffering, but a field of smiling faces and happy hearts."

★ ★ ★ ★ ★ ★ **MEMORIAL TO STAND ON** ★ ★ ★ ★ ★ ★

Union major general Daniel Sickles was injured while fighting at the Battle of Gettysburg in 1863. Army doctors decided his right leg had to be amputated if he was to live. Sickles agreed to the surgery, which at that time was a life-or-death operation, and managed to survive.

For years afterward, while other veterans visited the graves of fallen fighting companions, Sickles paid tribute to his lost leg—by visiting it at the Army Medical Museum! Soon after removing Sickles's leg, Army doctors decided to include it in an exhibit of Civil War medicine, perhaps because it belonged to such a high-ranking officer. The major general's leg is on display to this very day!

★ ★

THE SLAVE SONG JUBILEE

Americans everywhere have heard the soulful sound of gospel music, often sung in churches each Sunday morning. But did you know this music came from slave songs sung on Southern plantations—and only grew to popularity after the slaves were freed at the end of the Civil War?

After the war, thousands of schools were founded to educate newly freed African Americans, among them Nashville, Tennessee's, Fisk University. By 1871, however, five years after opening, Fisk was burdened by debt and in danger of closing its doors. George L. White, Fisk's treasurer, needed to find a way to raise money—and raise it fast. Fortunately, White was also the school's music teacher, and so the Jubilee Singers were born.

White selected nine of his students to join in a trip to the Northern states, "to sing the money out of the hearts and pockets of the people." Since seven of his pupils were former slaves, the group performed the slave songs they had grown up singing while working on Southern plantations. To church audiences throughout the North, these spiritual hymns were something new and deeply moving. When they were told that the Jubilee Singers were trying to raise money to save their school, people responded as White had hoped they would—by donating generously.

The group toured widely, traveling as far as Europe for their cause. Over the course of 7 years the singers succeeded in raising $150,000 to save Fisk University. "Never before," said a church minister who witnessed a performance, had he seen his congregation "so moved and melted by the magnetism of music."

UNION & CONFEDERATE SOLDIERS FOUGHT SIDE BY SIDE . . . IN EGYPT?

Some Civil War veterans, both Union and Confederate, were unwilling to lay down their guns at the declared end of war. Between 1876 and 1878 they joined together to continue the fight—in Egypt, Africa! How? Ismail Pasha, the man in charge of the Egyptian Army, wanted to modernize his country's military and gain independence from Turkey (which maintained responsibility for protecting Egypt at that time). With so many unemployed military leaders in America, the opportunity to recruit experienced soldiers seemed too great to pass up.

Pasha met with an ex-colonel in the Union cavalry named Thaddeus Mott, asking him to find as many American advisers as needed to train the Egyptian Army in the art of war. Each was promised $2,500 pay per year—in gold. In the end, 36 Union and Confederate officers joined the campaign.

Unfortunately, whatever dreams of glory these soldiers of fortune had in mind were not to be. The Civil War veterans found the Egyptian Army unable to adapt to the military discipline and tactics of a modern fighting force. The

Egyptians were soon beaten in battle by Abyssinian (Turkish) tribesmen. One of the American veterans described the whole adventure as "a miserable humbug—all show, all bunk, all make-believe."

★ ★ ★ ★ ★ ★ **"I SAW THE CIVIL WAR"** ★ ★ ★ ★ ★ ★

Most Americans witnessed the Civil War as ordinary citizens. Some of these ordinary citizens gained nationwide fame many years later:

★ As President Lincoln's funeral coffin paraded through New York City on April 25, 1865, two small boys watched from a second-floor window. One was 6-year-old Theodore Roosevelt, who would go on to become the nation's 26th president. The other was his brother Elliot, whose daughter Eleanor would one day marry Franklin Delano Roosevelt, America's 32nd president.

★ A band of Confederate guerrillas attacked and murdered 150 Kansas citizens who opposed the Southern cause in August of 1863. Among the unknown raiders was a young outlaw who would eventually gain fame throughout the west—Jesse James.

★ In March of 1862 the Union Army sent 10 scouts disguised as Confederate soldiers into Rebel-held territory in the west. The scout who reported back on the Confederate position was Captain James Butler Hickok—later known as Wild Bill Hickok, the famed cowboy.

★ One of the volunteer nurses tending the Yankees' wounded at the Union Hospital in Georgetown had just arrived in December of 1862 when a large group of soldiers from the Battle of Fredericksburg swamped the hospital's resources. Working amidst the bleeding troops and shattered limbs, the nurse contracted typhoid. She was taken home to Massachusetts and expected to die, but she survived and went on to write some of America's best-loved stories. The nurse was Louisa May Alcott, author of *Little Women*.

A DAY TO REMEMBER

Each year on May 30 Americans everywhere celebrate Memorial Day, a national holiday honoring deceased members of the armed forces . . . but did you know the tradition was actually begun by Confederate women?

After the war, a former Union general named John A. Logan became leader of the GAR (Grand Army of the Republic), a Union veteran's society. Logan remembered the old Southern custom of scattering flowers on the graves of dead soldiers. He thought it would be a good way for his society's members to parade together and honor their fellow Yankees. Logan picked May 30 as Memorial Day's official date simply because of the large number of flowers in bloom at that time of the year.

Confederate veterans, eager to continue a custom begun for their own soldiers, soon began celebrating Memorial Day— also called Decoration Day—on April 26, May 10, or June 3 instead. The dates varied depending upon each Southern state's own tradition.

THE CIVIL WAR & YOU

This book has explored the amazing places, people, and events of the Civil War. There are many ways you can further explore the war—through books, films, videos, CD-ROMs, the Internet, and by visiting actual Civil War memorials and battlegrounds. The following lists are but a few of the sources currently available. Become the Civil War expert in your neighborhood!

Note to parents: Due to the nature of war, some of these books contain mature themes that may be unsuitable for young children. Adult supervision is recommended in choosing material appropriate for your youngster.

BOOKS, FILMS & MORE

CIVIL WAR BOOKS

Fiction

The Red Badge of Courage
(Stephen Crane, 1895)
This is the story of Henry Fleming, a young, fearful Union soldier, and his experiences in battle. When he is injured, he earns his "red badge of courage."

Gone With the Wind
(Margaret Mitchell, 1936)
The story of Scarlett O'Hara,
a young Southern woman
growing up in Atlanta, Georgia,
at the beginning of the Civil
War. This is one of the most
famous stories about the Civil
War ever told.

The Last Silk Dress
(Ann Rinaldi, 1988)
Susan Chilmark is a young girl
from Richmond, Virginia, who
helps collect silk dresses from
Southern ladies to make a
Confederate spy balloon.

Nonfiction

A Separate Battle: Women and the Civil War
(Ina Chang, 1991)
Part of the *Young Readers' History of the Civil War* series, this book
tells the story of famous women who participated in the Civil War.

The Civil War Sourcebook: A Traveler's Guide
(Chuck Lawliss, 1991)
A compendium of Civil War historical sites, battlefields, memorials,
museums, and organizations throughout the United States. Included
are detailed listings of reenactment groups with addresses for
further information.

Don't Know Much About the Civil War
(Kenneth C. Davis, 1993)
An easy-to-read book covering all the important facts before, during,
and after the Civil War.

If You Lived at the Time of the Civil War
(Kay Moore, Annie Matsick—illustrator, 1994)
Learn what life was like for people living in either the North or the
South during the Civil War. Told with big color illustrations and
easy-to-read questions/answers.

The Victory Is Won: Black Soldiers in the Civil War
(Zak Mettger, 1994)
Part of the *Young Readers' History of the Civil War* series, this book shows the important role black Union soldiers played in helping to win the war.

The Civil War
(Martin W. Sandler, 1996)
More than 100 photos and illustrations from the Library of Congress in Washington, D.C., help tell the story of the Civil War and how it changed America.

The Complete Book of Confederate Trivia
(J. Stephen Lang, 1996)
Over 4,000 questions and answers on everything you ever wondered about the Confederate States of America.

CIVIL WAR FILMS & VIDEOS

The General
(Buster Keaton, 1926)
Buster Keaton tells a comedy version of the theft of the *General,* a Southern locomotive stolen by Union spies.

Gone With the Wind
(Vivien Leigh, Clark Gable, 1939)
The story of Southern belle Scarlett O'Hara's experiences living in Atlanta, Georgia, during the Civil War.

Young Mr. Lincoln
(Henry Fonda, 1939)
Abraham Lincoln is a young lawyer struggling to understand the difference between right and wrong.

Shenandoah
(James Stewart, 1965)
A Virginia man tries to ignore the Civil War, but events draw him and his family into the conflict.

Glory
(Matthew Broderick, Denzel Washington, 1989)
The story of the Union Army's 54th Massachusetts Regiment, assigned to attack Rebel soldiers at Fort Wagner, South Carolina. The 54th Massachusetts was the first all-black regiment to fight in the Civil War.

The Civil War
(PBS series, 1990)
Ken Burns's critically acclaimed series on the Civil War, told through photographs, letters, and interviews with historians.

Guns of the Civil War
(PBS series, 1996)
A television series about the amazing new weapons designed and used during the Civil War.

CIVIL WAR CD-ROMS

Civil War: America's Epic Struggle
(MultiEducator)
A narrated CD-ROM about the War Between the States, featuring thousands of photographs, illustrations, maps, and personal letters from many key participants.

The Civil War
(Scholastic)
A complete history of the Civil War, using photos, maps, and illustrations to trace the history of the conflict.

Civil War
(Quanta Press)
Biographies, statistics, weaponry, maps, and more are explored in this collection, along with period music performed by instruments from the Civil War era.

Twelve Roads to Gettysburg
(TDC Interactive)
A combination of animation, photographs, music, and narration tell the story of the Battle of Gettysburg, Pennsylvania.

CIVIL WAR WEBSITES*

The U.S. Civil War Center
http://www.cwc.lsu.edu/civlink.htm
An index of Civil War information available on the Internet, with
over 1,500 links to archives, special collections, films, games,
historical sites, reenactments, and more.

The Civil War WWW Information Archive
http://www.access.digex.net/~bdboyle/cw.html
A site providing information and links related to regiments, battles,
reenactments, and other Civil War groups.

Civil War Links Page
http://www.css.edu/mkelsey/civwar.html
A good starting point for links to other Civil War websites,
discussion groups, poetry, music, fiction, and more.

Civil War Photographs at the Library of Congress
http://lcweb2.loc.gov/ammem/cwphone.html
Part of the Library of Congress's "American Memory" exhibit, this is
a collection of hundreds of Civil War photographs covering all
aspects of the war.

Civil War Women
http://scriptorium.lib.duke.edu/collections/civil-war-women.html
An on-line archival exhibit at Duke University exploring the diaries
and letters of Southern women aiding the Confederacy.

U.S. Civil War Center-Reenactment Groups
http://reenact.org/home
A list of reenactment groups and activities in many different states,
with links for information and people to contact.

Tracing Your Civil War Ancestor
http://www.ancestry.com
A free ancestry search database can help you trace your roots back to
relatives who may have lived during or fought in the Civil War.

* All websites listed were active on date of publication.

A CIVIL WAR TRAVEL GUIDE

Abraham Lincoln Museum
Lincoln Memorial University Campus, Harrogate, Tennessee
(423) 869–3611
A research center and display gallery of more than 250,000 items relating to Abraham Lincoln and the Civil War.

Museum of the Confederacy
1201 East Clay Street, Richmond, Virginia
(804) 649–1861
The largest collection of Confederate artifacts in the nation.

Harriet Tubman Home
180 South Street, Auburn, New York
(315) 252–2081
Abolitionist Harriet Tubman's New York home, where she lived after escaping from slavery through the Underground Railroad.

Soldiers' National Monument
Gettysburg National Military Park, Gettysburg, Pennsylvania
(717) 334–1124
Commemorates the 3,700 Union dead who died at the Battle of Gettysburg.

Ford's Theater National Historic Site
511-516 10th Street, N.W., Washington, D.C.
(202) 426–6924
Site of President Lincoln's assassination by proslavery actor John Wilkes Booth. Nearby is Peterson house, where Lincoln was carried and died soon after being shot.

Lincoln Memorial
West Potomac Park at 23rd Street, N.W., Washington, D.C.
A dramatic memorial to the 16th president of the United States, featuring events and memorabilia from Abraham Lincoln's life and legacy.

CIVIL WAR NATIONAL PARKS

America's National Parks Service oversees the preservation of the country's historic battlegrounds. It offers tours to visitors and presents information that keeps the memory of the Civil War alive. Some selected Civil War parks include:

Fort Sumter National Monument
1214 Middle Street, Sullivans Island, SC 29482
The site of the first shots of the Civil War.

Manassas National Battlefield Park
6511 Sudley Road, Manassas, VA 22110
The Union Army saw two major defeats at Manassas, nearly a year apart.

Shiloh National Military Park
P.O. Box 67, Shiloh, TN 38376
Shiloh, Tennessee was the scene of the first major battle as the Civil War began to spread west.

Antietam National Battlefield
P.O. Box 158, Sharpsburg, MD 21782
Antietam, Maryland, was the scene of the bloodiest single day's battle of the entire war.

Gettysburg National Military Park
P.O. Box 1080, Gettysburg, PA 17325
The three-day battle at Gettysburg, Pennsylvania, was the largest and bloodiest battle of the Civil War. It marked the beginning of the Union's drive toward victory.

Andersonville National Historic Site
Route 1, Box 800, Andersonville, GA 31711
The Confederate camp at Andersonville is remembered as the scene of great cruelty and suffering for the Union soldiers imprisoned there.

Appomattox Court House National Historic Park
P.O. Box 218, Appomattox, VA 24522
The site of Confederate general Robert E. Lee's final surrender to Union general Ulysses S. Grant.

SEE THE CIVIL WAR YOURSELF!

How would you like to travel back in time and see the Civil War—or even take part in it yourself? You can! Each year, a variety of historic preservation societies stage live reenactments of famous Civil War battles, complete with authentic reproductions of costumes, weaponry, and more. Sign up as a regiment's drummer boy—or girl! Pick up a musket and take part in a battle. (Real bullets are not used.)

Many of America's Civil War battlefields stage reenactments. For further information, contact each National Battlefield individually. In addition, many Civil War magazines list advertisements for various reenactment groups, with sources for further information.

A calendar of events, locations, and contact information can also be found on-line at the U.S. Civil War Center-Reenactment Groups website:

http://www.cwc.lsu.edu/other/reenact.rgroup.htm

Ask for the location of a Civil War reenactment group near you!

CIVIL WAR CHRONOLOGY

1619
- 1st slaves to America land in Virginia

1652
- Rhode Island declares slavery illegal

1688
- 1st public protest of slave trade in Pennsylvania

1700
- Virginia declares slaves are "property"
- New York puts runaway slaves to death

1725
- Virginia grants slaves right to form own church

1739
- Slave rebellion in South Carolina; 44 slaves killed

1754
- Quaker John Woolman preaches against slavery

1777
- Vermont outlaws slavery

1783
- Massachusetts outlaws slavery

1792
- Kentucky joins Union as slave state

1793
- The Fugitive Slave Act forces return of runaway slaves

1796
- Tennessee joins Union as slave state

1800
- Free blacks petition Congress to end slavery
- Armed slaves rebel in Virginia; most are executed

1803
- Ohio joins Union as free state
- U.S. buys Louisiana Territory, fueling debate over slave status

1808
- Congress outlaws slave trade; slavery persists

1812
- Louisiana joins Union as slave state

1816
- Indiana joins Union as free state

1817
- Mississippi joins Union as slave state

1818
- Illinois joins Union as free state

1819
- Alabama joins Union as slave state

1820
- The Missouri Compromise admits Maine to Union as free state, Missouri as slave state, and prohibits slavery north of Missouri

1822
- Slaves revolt in South Carolina; 37 are hanged

1827
- New York outlaws slavery

1828
- South Carolina insists states can void federal laws

1830
- Congress debates states' rights vs. federal government

1831
- Abolitionist William Lloyd Garrison publishes *The Liberator*
- Slave rebellion in Virginia leads to tougher slave laws

1832
- Congress passes new tariff law, benefiting Northern industry
- South Carolina nullifies federal edict, calls for secession
- President Jackson declares no states may leave Union

1833
- Lucretia Mott forms Female Anti-Slavery Society
- Theodore Weld forms American Anti-Slavery Society
- Ohio's Oberlin College 1st to admit blacks

1835
- South Carolina burns abolitionist literature
- Georgia threatens to enact death penalty for abolitionist writers
- Abolitionist William Ellery Channing publishes *Slavery*

1836
- Arkansas joins Union as slave state

1837
- Michigan joins Union as free state

1845
- Florida joins Union as slave state
- Texas joins Union as slave state

1848
- Wisconsin joins Union as free state

1850
- Congress passes the Compromise of 1850
- Southern states declare right to secede if Compromise is broken

1852
- Harriet Beecher Stowe publishes *Uncle Tom's Cabin*
- Proslavery candidate Franklin Pierce elected president

1853
- Jefferson Davis joins Pierce administration as war secretary

1854
- Congress passes the Kansas-Nebraska Act, overturning Missouri Compromise; settlers in Kansas-Nebraska Territory battle over free-state or slave-state status

1855
- Proslavery forces declare victory in Kansas
- Separate election by free-state Kansans produce two legislatures

1856
- Proslavery candidate James Buchanan elected president

1857
- Supreme Court rules escaped slave Dred Scott is property that must be returned to owner
- Congress battles over Kansas's status as a free state or a slave state

1858
- Minnesota joins Union as free state
- Illinois candidates Abraham Lincoln and Stephen Douglas debate issues of slavery; Douglas wins election to Senate

1859
- Oregon joins Union as free state
- Arkansas forces free blacks to leave state
- Southern States' Convention proposes reinstating slave trade
- Abolitionist John Brown leads slave revolt; Brown is hanged

1860
- Antislavery candidate Abraham Lincoln elected president
- South Carolina votes to secede from the Union

1861
- Florida, Alabama, Georgia, Mississippi, and Louisiana secede from Union
- Kansas joins Union as free state
- Southern states form Confederate States of America
- Jefferson Davis elected Confederate president
- Texas secedes; joins Confederacy
- South Carolina troops attack Federal Fort Sumter
- Federal Navy blockades Southern ports
- Virginia, Tennessee, and North Carolina join Confederacy
- Union defeated at Battle of Bull Run
- Union defeated at Battle of Ball's Bluff
- Lincoln replaces Union general Winfield Scott with General George B. McClellan

1862
- Union Army captures Nashville, Tennessee
- 1st ironclad ship battle between *Monitor* and *Merrimac*
- Union's Army of the Potomac begins new offensive against South
- At Battle of Shiloh, Ulysses S. Grant forces Rebel troops to retreat
- Seven Day's Battle forces Army of the Potomac to retreat
- 2nd Battle of Bull Run ends in Union defeat
- Battle of Antietam becomes bloodiest day of the Civil War
- 1st black regiment formed
- Confederate troops defeated at Battle of Perryville
- Union forces defeated at Battle of Fredericksburg
- No ground gained on either side at Battle of Murfreesboro

1863
- President Lincoln issues Emancipation Proclamation
- Union War Department establishes Bureau of Colored Troops
- Union forces defeated at Battle of Chancellorsville

- Confederate general Thomas "Stonewall" Jackson killed
- Grant conquers Vicksburg, Mississippi
- Union gains control of Mississippi River
- West Virginia joins Union as free state
- Battle of Gettysburg begins to turn tide of war for Union
- Confederate Army forces Union retreat at Battle of Chickamauga
- Union forces Confederacy retreat at Battle of Chattanooga
- Lincoln gives Gettysburg Address
- Union forces control Tennessee

1864
- Grant appointed commander of Union Army
- No ground gained on either side at Battle of the Wilderness
- No progress on either side at Battle of Spotsylvania Court House
- Grant drives Union forces to Richmond, the Confederate capital
- General Sherman conquers Atlanta, Georgia
- Maryland abolishes slavery
- Nevada joins Union as free state
- Abraham Lincoln wins reelection as president
- Sherman begins "March to the Sea" along Georgia coastline
- Confederates defeated at Battle of Franklin, Tennessee
- Confederates defeated at Battle of Nashville

1865
- Missouri abolishes slavery
- Abraham Lincoln rejects Jefferson Davis's peace proposals
- 13th Amendment to the Constitution abolishes slavery
- Union Army enters Richmond, Virginia

- Confederacy forced into full retreat at Battle of Sayler's Creek
- Confederate general Robert E. Lee surrenders to Union general Ulysses S. Grant at Appomattox Court House, Virginia
- President Lincoln assassinated by Southerner John Wilkes Booth
- Vice President Andrew Johnson sworn into office
- John Wilkes Booth shot and killed in Bowling Green, Virginia
- President Johnson submits plan for Restoration of South
- All Confederate states except Mississippi readmitted to Union
- Six Confederate officers form antiblack society, Ku Klux Klan

1866
- Congress passes Civil Rights Act

1868
- 14th Amendment to the Constitution guarantees equal rights

1870
- 15th Amendment grants blacks right to vote

INDEX

abolition of slavery, 6, 7, 20
aftermath of war, 93–102
American Indians, 52, 68–69
Anaconda Plan, 29
army life, 56–57
Arthur, Chester A., 108

Barringer, Rufus, 62–63
Barton, Clara, 71–72
Battle of Gettysburg, 89–90, 91–92, 111–112
battles, 39–44
black soldiers, 50–52
Bloomer, Amelia, 16
Booth, John Wilkes, 27, 93–94
Boyd, Belle, 76
boy soldiers, 53–55, 56

chronology, 124–127
Civil War, other names for, 9, 53
civil wars, 4–5, 8–9
Clem, Johnny, 53–55
coding system, 83
Compromise of 1850, 20–21
Confederacy, defined, 5
Confederate Army, 25, 27–28, 47–48, 52, 53, 56–63, 64, 65, 67
Constitutional amendments, 98, 99, 102, 104
Custer, George Armstrong, 35–36

Davis, Jefferson, 18, 27–28, 87–88, 95
Declaration of Independence, 5–6
disabled soldiers, 55–56
Dix, Dorothea, 70–71
Douglas, Stephen A., 22, 25
Douglass, Frederick, 51
Dred Scott decision, 21
Durnford, Andrew, 13

Emancipation Proclamation, 26, 50, 51

Europe, 45, 69–70
everyday life, 10–17

Fife and Drummer Corps, 53–54
flags, 77–78
foreign soldiers, 69–70
Fort Sumter, 24, 25, 37–38
free states, 6

Garfield, James A., 108
Gettysburg Address, 90
Grant, Ulysses S., 26, 30–31, 93, 108

Harrison, Benjamin, 109
Hayes, Rutherford B., 102, 108

income taxes, 91
information resources, 116–123
inventions, 78–85, 103
issues leading to Civil War, 5–7, 18

Jackson, "Stonewall," 34–35, 59
Johnson, Andrew, 28, 95, 96, 97, 98, 107

Kansas–Nebraska Act, 22–23
Ku Klux Klan, 101

Lee, Robert E., 32–33, 60, 62, 93, 95, 110–111
Lincoln, Abraham, 12, 16, 24–27, 62–63, 90, 93–94

McClean, Wilmer, 46–47
McKinley, William, 109
manufacturing, 17, 19
Memorial Day, 115
Missouri Compromise, 19–20
Mundy, Sue, 67
music, 53–54, 61–62, 92, 112–113

Northerners, 6, 17–18, 24

plantations, 6, 17
Pony Express, 14–15
postwar years, 93–106

Reconstruction, 99–100, 102
Revels, Hiram, 105–106
Ruffin, Edmund, 37–38

schools, 10–11
Scott, Dred, 21
Scott, Winfield, 29–30
secession, 25, 32, 37
Sherman, William Tecumseh, 26, 33–34, 59
slavery, 6, 13–14, 21, 23, 52
slavery, abolishment of, 6, 7, 20, 101–102, 105
soldiers, 47–63, 86–87
Southerners, 6–7, 18–19, 24, 25, 28
spies, 63–64, 68, 74–76, 83
Stevens, Thaddeus, 98–99
Stowe, Harriet Beecher, 23
supply wagons, 58–59
surrender, 33, 93, 95

Transcontinental Railroad, 14, 15
travel, 11–12
Tubman, Harriet, 72–73

Uncle Tom's Cabin (Stowe), 23
Underground Railroad, 73
Union Army, 29, 47–64, 65–67, 97
U.S. Sanitary Commission, 72, 89

Van Lew, Elizabeth, 74–75
veterans, 55–56, 113–114, 115
voting rights, 98, 101–102, 104

Washington, D.C., 55–56, 85–86, 97
weapons, 79–84
Webster, Timothy, 63–64
women, 23, 67, 70–76, 104

Yankees, defined, 5